MW01295551

Facts & Furious

Facts & Furious
The Facts About America and Why They Make the Left Furious

Ben Shapiro

Creators Publishing
Hermosa Beach, CA

FACTS & FURIOUS
Copyright © 2024 CREATORS PUBLISHING
All rights reserved. No part of this book may be reproduced or transmitted in any form or by any means, electronic or mechanical, including photocopying, recording or by any information storage and retrieval system, without permission in writing from the author.

Cover art by Coral Black

CREATORS PUBLISHING
737 3rd St
Hermosa Beach, CA 90254
310-337-7003

Although the author and publisher have made every effort to ensure that the information in this book was correct at press time, the author and publisher do not assume and hereby disclaim any liability to any party for any loss, damage or disruption caused by errors or omissions, whether such errors or omissions result from negligence, accident or any other cause.

ISBN (print): 978-1-962693-13-4
ISBN (ebook): 978-1-962693-14-1

First Edition
Printed in the United States of America
1 3 5 7 9 10 8 6 4 2

Contents

Road to the Election

The Democrats' Exploitation of Jan. 6 Gives Away Their Game

January 5, 2022

This year, Jan. 6 will be commemorated with all the ballyhoo and rigamarole Democrats and their media allies can muster. CNN plans an entire special around the anniversary, titled "Live from the Capitol: January 6th, One Year Later"; the show will feature the "heroes who protected our democracy in the face of an insurrection," and will include interviews with such luminaries as House Speaker Nancy Pelosi, D-Calif., and January 6 Committee Chair Bennie Thompson, D-Miss. President Joe Biden and Vice President Kamala Harris are also expected to commemorate Jan. 6 with special remarks, and Pelosi has organized a bevy of events in memory of the riot.

Now, you might ask yourself just why Jan. 6 merits such outsized attention. One need not downplay the events—the horrifying image of rioters bashing police officers with metal poles, storming through the halls of Congress shouting for Mike Pence—in order to recognize Jan. 6 for what it was: an ugly but not pivotal moment in American history. The event resulted in one direct death—rioter Ashli Babbitt was shot by a Capitol police officer—and some $1.5 million in property damage to the Capitol building; the Capitol was cleared within hours of the riot, and Vice President Mike Pence and Senate Majority Leader Mitch McConnell promptly presided over the certification of the 2020 election. Those who broke into the Capitol or even trespassed have ended up in jail.

Meanwhile, by contrast, the Black Lives Matter riots of 2020 resulted in some $2 billion in insured property damage (and likely billions more in uninsured property damage), two dozen people died, and the resultant political movement against the police led to an unprecedented nationwide spike in homicides in major cities. To date, there have been no commemorations from CNN, speeches from Biden or Harris, or a day honoring the police officers who held rioters in check.

So, what lies behind the Democratic-media obsession with Jan. 6? Political opportunism. Democrats aren't even hiding the ball. Facing the ever-likelier prospect of a 2022 midterm wipeout, Democrats have hit on a strategy: they have to rig the electoral rules and overthrow traditional democratic institutions in order to stop Republicans from rigging the electoral rules and overthrowing traditional democratic institutions. Jan. 6, to opportunistic Democrats, is the all-purpose excuse to use the entire weight of their party to push for a radical revision of Senate rules and federal elections. As Politico reported this week, "Democrats are hoping that Thursday will be more than just a day of remembrance. In the Senate, we hear from well-positioned sources, there's a desire to take the opportunity to supercharge the party's long-stalled voting rights legislation—possibly even using the anniversary to try to get Sens. Krysten Sinema, D-Ariz., and Joe Manchin, D-W.Va, to go nuclear on the filibuster or embrace rules changes."

Yes, the electoral village must be burned in order to stop future events similar to Jan. 6. As The New York Times editorialized, "Every Day Is January 6 Now," arguing, "the Capitol riot continues in statehouses across the country, in a bloodless, legalized form that no police officer can arrest and that no prosecutor can try in court." The only plausible response is to federalize election procedures constitutionally given to the states, to mandate the corrupt practice of ballot harvesting, to mandate long periods of early voting and universal absentee ballots, to loosen voter verification, and much more.

All because of Jan. 6.

Or, perhaps, because Democrats can read the writing on the wall. They know that November 2022 cometh, and that right soon. And they hope that if they invoke the specter of Jan. 6 repeatedly, Americans will shrug and allow them to usurp authority, violate rules, and rewrite voting procedure. It won't work. But it should reveal to Americans just who Democrats are, and how little they actually care about Jan. 6 in the first place.

The Day the FBI Raided Donald Trump

August 10, 2022

This week, the FBI raided the Florida home of former President Donald Trump at Mar-a-Lago. They based their raid on the purported rationale that they suspected Trump of having mishandled classified information, taking home materials meant for the National Archives: according to The New York Times, the search "appeared to be focused on material that Mr. Trump had brought with him to Mar-a-Lago ... Those boxes contained many pages of classified documents." Trump quickly responded with outrage: "After working and cooperating with the relevant Government agencies, this unannounced raid on my home was not necessary or appropriate. Such an assault could only take place in broken, Third-World Countries. They even broke into my safe!"

We have not yet seen the warrant for the raid, the warrant application or the underlying evidence; presumably, the head of the FBI and the head of the Department of Justice, Attorney General Merrick Garland, would have had to sign off on the raid. And, to put it mildly, the basis for such a raid—a raid authorized by a current presidential administration on the leader of the prior administration and front-runner for the nomination in 2024—seems extraordinarily weak. In 2015, former Clinton national security adviser Sandy Berger only received a misdemeanor charge for stuffing classified documents down his pants; in 2016, the FBI investigated Hillary Clinton's mishandling of classified emails but certainly never raided her home or offices, despite finding that it was "possible that hostile actors gained access to Secretary Clinton's personal e-mail account," complete with access to classified information. Trump, by contrast, was *president*—which means he had plenary authority to declassify any document. Yet it was Trump who was raided.

If the basis for the raid is anything less than bedrock-solid, therefore, the most serious questions of political legitimacy will be on the table. After all, this amounts to the current administration authorizing a raid on the head of the prior administration; it apparently centers on a matter unrelated to events surrounding Jan. 6 and the aftermath of the 2020 election. It seems, on its face, pretextual. We won't know whether it is or isn't until we see the underlying documentation. But without the sort of trust the FBI has failed to cultivate over the past few years, the clamor for such documentation will rightly be deafening.

Suspicions are certainly in order, given the behavior of the FBI over the course of the last few years. The FBI spent years running a deep investigation on Trump's campaign and presidency, based on speculative nonsense compiled by the Clinton campaign in the form of the so-called Steele dossier. FBI Director James Comey seemed to launder that nonsense into the press by presenting Trump with the dossier, despite no evidence that the dossier had any support whatsoever. There is a reason that as of 2018, just 45% of independents and 39% of Republicans said they trusted the FBI most or all of the time.

The FBI raid on Trump could easily be yet another inflection point in the complete breakdown of America's public institutions. Every "I" must be dotted and "t" crossed—and there must be tangible results. Anything less should and will lead to a political crisis of real magnitude.

Joe Biden Is the Real Semi-Fascist

August 31, 2022

This week, President Joe Biden—in search of a new label to pin on his political opponents after the failure of his "ultra-MAGA" branding, which prompted peals of laughter rather than shudders of horror—landed on a new slur with which to tar those who don't support his agenda: they are, he said, semi-fascists. Speaking with a crowd of Democratic donors in Maryland, Biden reportedly said, "What we're seeing now is either the beginning or the death knell of an extreme MAGA philosophy. It's not just Trump, it's the entire philosophy that underpins the—I'm going to say something—it's semi-fascism."

Now, Democratic politicians painting half of Americans as beneath contempt is old hat. Former President Barack Obama, of course, said that Americans who didn't support him in 2008 were merely bitter bigots, clinging to "guns or religion or antipathy toward people who aren't like them." Hillary Clinton was more pithy: she called them a "basket of deplorables." So, "semi-fascist" shouldn't come as much of a shock.

But that smear is particularly galling coming from Biden the same week in which he announced, without any constitutional authority whatsoever, that he was erasing some $500 billion in student loan debts—the single largest executive action in American history. Biden justified that action on the basis of a nonexistent COVID-19 emergency. He has justified similar usurpations on similar grounds: He illegally tasked his Occupational Safety and Health Administration with forcing vaccines on some 80 million people on the basis of a "public health emergency"; he used his Centers for Disease Control and Prevention to try to propagate an eviction moratorium on the same basis; he bragged in July that he will reshape the American economy on his own if Congress doesn't act in order to forestall a supposed "climate change emergency."

If we're talking about semi-fascism, this stuff qualifies.

The history of fascism, after all, does not begin with a dictator simply marching into a nation's capital and seizing total power. It more frequently begins with the destruction of the legislative branch at the hands of centralization of executive power. Adolf Hitler didn't just declare himself dictator; dictatorial power preceded him in the chancellor's office by several years, dating back to Heinrich Bruning invoking emergency powers under Article 48 of the Weimar Constitution in 1930. Benito Mussolini came to power under constitutional means in 1922 and didn't consolidate his rule until 1925. Fascism, in other words, is a gradual process. And that process starts with executive branch actors accreting authority they were never given.

Because our political discourse has devolved into middle-school histrionics—"Everyone I don't like is Hitler!"—we fail to notice the gradual slide into tyranny, ignoring it on behalf of spectacular headlines and reactionary rhetoric. Standing up to that process isn't semi-fascism; it's the opposite.

American Democracy Isn't in Peril—So Long as Americans Talk to Each Other

October 19, 2022

American democracy, we have been told, is in grave peril.

It's a perspective we hear echoed dozens of times per day in the mainstream media: If this next election doesn't go precisely how our hallowed elitists desire, surely tyranny will follow. As one of those sagacious experts, MSNBC's Joy Reid, recently put it on Twitter, "It's terrifying how many Americans will choose literal fascism, female serfdom, climate collapse and the reversal of everything from Social Security & Medicare to student loan relief bc they think giving Republicans the power to investigate Hunter Biden will bring down gas prices."

Polls show that this message has filtered down to many Americans, mostly Democrats. According to the latest New York Times/Sienna poll, fully 11% of Democrats say "the state of our democracy" is the most important problem facing the country, compared with 17% who cite the economy and another 17% who cite inflation; 9% of independents feel the same way. More shocking, just 46% of Americans say that "America's political system can still address the nation's problems," compared with 48% who say that the nation is "too divided politically to solve its problems." And fully 74% of likely voters say American democracy is currently under threat.

All of which imply we should be pretty damned worried about the state of the republic.

And yet when we drill down, we see broad agreement among Americans that their neighbors aren't their enemies; that our institutions are worth upholding; that the only remedy for our current political ills is to continue to work within the constitutional system.

According to that same poll, just 20% of voters say they've had a disagreement with family or friends over politics that hurt their relationship; just 14% say that someone's political views "tell you a lot about whether someone is a good person"; just 30% say that presidents should violate the laws to pursue "what they think is best."

Just 14% of likely voters say we will need to "go outside the law" to fix our democracy—16% of Democrats, 15% of independents and 9% of Republicans. Even among those who say we must "go outside the law," just 12% say Americans should take up arms or participate in violence—meaning just 1.7% of likely voters advocate civil war. Meanwhile, 84% of likely voters say we can fix our democracy without destroying the system.

As for the media's favorite Trumpian conspiracy theory, QAnon, just 5% of likely voters call the theory believable.

So, why precisely *are* so many Americans worried about the state of democracy? They're worried that their political opponents will threaten the institutions they cherish. Forty-seven percent of voters declare former President Donald Trump a "major threat to democracy," and 39% declare President Joe Biden to be the same. But shockingly, the institution they blame most for threatening democracy is the mainstream media, with 59% of likely voters, including 54% of independents, calling the mainstream media a "major threat to democracy."

Perhaps that's the biggest takeaway from all this data: that Americans don't hate each other, but they're being polarized by a media determined to divide them from one another, whipping up madness where mere concern would suffice. And what's more, Americans can feel it.

All of which means that sanity may reign once again, so long as Americans reconnect with each other rather than believing everything they see on the news.

The Red Fizzle

November 9, 2022

There was no red wave. There was no red tide. There was no red trickle.

There was a fizzle.

The 2022 midterm election fundamentals would have suggested a ringing Republican victory: an unpopular president of the opposing party, deep public unhappiness with the state of the economy, unified Democratic control in Congress and radical social policy out of step with most Americans. Polls showed Republicans cutting deeply into Democratic constituencies including Hispanic and black voting blocs.

Yet as of Wednesday morning, Republicans, who were widely expected to win historic margins in the House of Representatives and to take back the United States Senate, are coming up short nearly everywhere. They will likely take back the House, but by a slim margin after an extraordinarily tepid showing that may land them with a majority of just north of 220 seats; they are unlikely to take back the Senate, given that the deciding vote will likely come via a runoff in a Georgia Senate race featuring the highly vulnerable and troubled candidacy of Herschel Walker.

So, what happened?

What happened is that in many districts and states all over the country, Republicans picked bad candidates. Believing that the fundamentals were all that was necessary to sweep them to victory, Republican leadership failed to intervene in these primaries to the extent necessary to ensure durable general election candidates. They stood aside largely out of fear of former President Donald Trump; Trump himself personally intervened in a variety of cases in the primaries, endorsing candidates almost solely on the basis of whether they were sufficiently sycophantic regarding the election of 2020.

Those candidates then lost.

And then Trump ripped them. Take, for example, Don Bolduc in New Hampshire. New Hampshire is a toss-up state; late polls suggested that Bolduc, despite his myriad oddities and strong support for Trump's 2020 election fraud claims, might win the race. Instead, he lost by double digits. And Trump promptly took to Truth Social to let the world know that Bolduc deserved it: "Don Bolduc was a very nice guy, but he lost tonight when he disavowed, after his big primary win, his longstanding stance on Election Fraud in the 2020 Presidential Primary. Had he stayed strong and true, he would have own easily. Lessons Learned!!!" He also took the time to issue a statement *celebrating* a Democrat winning the Colorado Senate seat, ripping Republican Joe O'Dea, who had refused to countenance Trump's election 2020 obsession: "Joe O'Dea lost BIG! MAKE AMERICA GREAT AGAIN!"

The Republican Party had one job in the 2022 election cycle: to provide some semblance of responsible leadership. Where they didn't, they lost.

And where they did, they won.

In Florida, Gov. Ron DeSantis, who reopened the state during COVID-19, ensured children could go to school unmasked, kept the economy open, handled Hurricane Ian and fought off the predations of wokesters and corporate Left-wingers, won an overwhelming victory: he grew his 30,000-vote, 0.4% 2018 victory margin to *1.5 million votes and nearly 20 points,* and took the entire Florida GOP along for the ride. Republicans picked up four House seats in the state; Marco Rubio defeated Val Demings in the Senate by over 16 points, and won the Hispanic vote outright, taking even historically blue Miami-Dade County.

Meanwhile, Trump was taking potshots at "Ron DeSanctimonious."

In Georgia, Gov. Brian Kemp handily defeated Democratic darling Stacey Abrams, despite Trump's personal attempts to defeat Kemp in his primary—again, due to Kemp's failure to illegally flip the state to Trump in the 2020 election. Kemp is trusted by Georgians; he won.

There is a silver lining here for Republicans. Democrats, who should have been taught a lesson by voters, were saved by Republican incompetence and pusillanimity; that means they'll keep doubling down. President Joe Biden is, barring actual incapacity, the prohibitive 2024 Democratic nominee. And the fundamentals will continue to move against Democrats as they pursue a woker and woker agenda.

This means Republicans will get another bite at the apple—but only if they get serious. The time for frivolity is over. The laws of political gravity apply. Nominate good, sober candidates capable of governing and earning the trust of Americans. Pick your culture war battles and hit them hard. Make it hard to vote for Democrats and easy to vote for you.

This isn't tough stuff. But if Republican leadership is unwilling to pursue the obvious, the shipwreck of 2022 will be only the beginning.

The Trump-DeSantis Primary Fight Begins

March 22, 2023

This week, as Manhattan District Attorney Alvin Bragg considered indicting former President Donald Trump on a flimsy felony charge over a seven-year-old hush-money payment to former porn star Stormy Daniels, Trump placed his focus on the man he perceives as the truest threat to his political dominance: Florida Gov. Ron DeSantis. Trump backers demanded that DeSantis sound off on the looming indictment; after a few days, DeSantis did, but not in ways that pleased Trump's base. "I don't know what goes into paying hush money to a porn star to secure silence over some type of alleged affair," DeSantis said. "But what I can speak to is if you have a prosecutor who is ignoring crimes happening every single day in his jurisdiction and he chooses to go back many, many years ago to try to use something about porn star hush money payments, that's an example of pursuing a political agenda."

DeSantis' harsh words for Bragg were insufficient, according to Trump, because he mentioned the rationale for Trump's legal difficulties: his unfortunate penchant for sexual profligacy. This prompted Trump to take to Truth Social to accuse DeSantis of grooming underage girls and/or boys: "Ron DeSanctimonious will probably find out about FALSE ACCUSATIONS & FAKE STORIES sometime in the future, as he gets older, wiser, and better known, when he's unfairly and illegally attacked by a woman, even classmates that are 'underage' (or possibly a man!)."

This was only the beginning. On Tuesday evening, excerpts broke from a DeSantis interview with Piers Morgan, in which DeSantis criticized Trump's choices as president. "(T)he way we run the government I think is no daily drama, focus on the big picture and put points on the board and I think that's something that's very important," DeSantis said. He added that he "would have fired" Dr.

Anthony Fauci, contra Trump, who made Fauci into the face of the federal government's pandemic response.

So, the fight is on.

Right now, the advantage lies with Trump. He's the center of gravity for all of politics. DeSantis led Trump 39% to 26% in the Monmouth poll in December 2022—shortly after Trump's candidates in Senate races lost across the board, while DeSantis cleaned up in Florida—but now trails Trump by a margin of 27% to 41% in the same poll.

Dealing with Trump will be difficult for any Republican candidate, for two specific reasons. First, many Republican voters have bought into the myth that Trump is not subject to political gravity: In the aftermath of the 2012 Obama reelection, widespread political sentiment held that Democrats would never lose another presidential election, and yet Trump somehow beat Hillary Clinton while saying anything and everything on his mind. Many Republicans still think of Trump as a winner, even after his losses in the 2018 midterm election, 2020 presidential election, 2021 Georgia Senate races and 2022 midterms. When they don't, he drops in the polls, as in December 2022.

Second, Republicans rally to Trump whenever he is attacked by the Left. That's right and proper when it comes to unjust prosecutions by rogue DAs. But many Republican voters have generalized to the extent that Trump is now considered off-limits to attack even by *other Republicans,* since the Left *might* use such attacks as a rationale to attack Trump, too. This is a nearly impossible needle to thread. How do you critique Trump without the base feeling that your attacks are helping the Left? Meanwhile, Trump has been granted the soft bigotry of low expectations by many voters: He can say literally anything about other candidates, and no one blinks an eye. It's Marquess of Queensberry rules for Trump's opponents, WWE folding-chair-to-the-back-of-the-head smackdowns for Trump himself.

So, what can DeSantis do? The answer: It's not really up to DeSantis. It's up to Republican voters. It will be DeSantis' job to remind Republican voters that Trump has won precisely one election in the last seven years; it will be the job of Republican voters to acknowledge that reality. It will be DeSantis' job to point out that

Trump didn't clean out the executive branch and gave Fauci power; it will be the job of Republican voters to acknowledge that such criticisms aren't "unfair attacks." It will be DeSantis' job to remind voters of his record; it will be the job of Republican voters to look to record rather than tweetstorms for policy victory.

Will Republican voters use their heads rather than their hearts? We'll find out soon enough.

Joe Biden Threatens To 'Finish the Job'

April 26, 2023

This week, President Joe Biden formally launched his 2024 reelection campaign. He did so with a three-minute video in which he did not appear on camera speaking for more than two seconds at a time; the highly produced video instead utilizes audio of Biden over fast cuts of Normal Americans (TM) doing Normal Things (TM). Biden's message is simple: "Finish the Job."

But what, precisely, is the job? Biden's first term record is abysmal: a 40-year inflation high, now baked into the price structure; systemic weakness in the banking system, brought about by the necessity of the Federal Reserve raising interest rates; an out-of-control debt problem that will only appreciate over time; a collapsing Middle East in which a serious war is now the most likely outcome; an emboldened China casting its eyes upon Taiwan; a Europe unsure about American leadership despite the war in Ukraine; an Afghanistan turned over to eighth-century barbarians, with hundreds of Americans still behind enemy lines and 13 American service members murdered; and a social fabric frayed beyond recognition by the insistence on racial "equity" and the false malleability of sex itself, especially for children.

Biden's record is one of the worst for any first-term president. His "Finish the Job" slogan sounds more like a threat by a movie villain than a guarantee of future prosperity.

Joe Biden has nothing to run on.

Nothing except former President Donald Trump.

His announcement contains zero actual accomplishments of his first term. Instead, his entire campaign will be rooted in the same message as his first campaign, and the Democrats' 2022 campaign: Vote against Republicans—and by Republicans, they mean Trump—or democracy will be imperiled. "That's been the work of our first term," Biden intones. "To fight for our democracy ... But, you know, around the country, MAGA extremists are lining up to take on these bedrock freedoms." By MAGA extremists, of course, Biden doesn't just mean people who attempted to prevent certification of the 2020 election. He means anyone who opposes his agenda. "When I ran for president four years ago," Biden mumbles, "I said we were in a battle for the soul of America. And we still are."

This campaign strategy rests almost entirely on Republicans nominating Trump. In 2022, this message resonated only in areas that nominated Trump-lite candidates, from Georgia to Pennsylvania to New Hampshire. In New York and Florida, where Republicans ran more traditional Republican candidates, Democrats lost seats. Gov. Brian Kemp, who did not bow to Trump's pressure in Georgia, won reelection handily; so did Gov. Ron DeSantis in Florida, who ran on his record of accomplishment and freedom in the state. Democrats' "Democracy Dies in Darkness" sloganeering only carries weight when Republicans allow it to do so.

Will Republicans hand the 2024 election to Biden? They very well could. Right now, Trump leads in the Republican primaries, despite attacking his nearest rival, DeSantis, almost entirely from the Left: bashing DeSantis' record on COVID-19, slamming entitlement reform, criticizing DeSantis' battle against Disney's corporate social engineering. Trump has been unfairly targeted by political opponents to be sure—Manhattan DA Alvin Bragg's case against Trump over a 2016 payoff to former porn star Stormy Daniels is a legal joke. But that doesn't mean that Republicans are likely to benefit from a campaign revolving around Trump's legal troubles and his persistent focus on the supposedly "stolen" 2020 election. In fact, Trump has yet to answer the most basic question he himself has raised about his electability: If, as he states, the 2020 election was stolen through voter fraud and falsification, how does he plan to overcome that problem in the 2024 election?

The polls show a consistent pattern: If Trump is the Republican candidate, Biden is more likely to win. It is difficult to imagine millions of Americans switching their 2020 votes in precisely the opposite direction. Indeed, polls currently show Biden beating Trump by an average of 3.1%, while losing to DeSantis by a slim margin. Trump currently trails Biden—a president with an approval rating in the low 40s—in Arizona, Michigan, Nevada, North Carolina, Pennsylvania and Wisconsin.

Joe Biden wants Trump. His entire campaign is built around Trump. Perhaps, like Hillary Clinton, he'll get more than he bargained for. But Republicans don't need to take that gamble. And they're clearly running a higher risk of a Biden second term if they do.

How CNN Just Boosted Trump

May 10, 2023

This week, former President Donald Trump appeared on a CNN town hall. That day, he trumpeted the upcoming event on his social media platforms. "I'll be doing CNN tonight live from the great state of New Hampshire because CNN is rightfully desperate to get those Trump ratings back," Trump said with a wry grin. "They were ratings like none other, and they want them back. They made me a deal they couldn't refuse. It could be the beginning of a new and vibrant CNN with no more fake news, or it could be a total disaster for all, including me. Let's see what happens, tonight at 8 o'clock!"

Trump pitched the event like a WWE Monday Night Raw.

And it was.

It was kayfabe of the highest order. And it helped Trump immensely.

CNN pitched the event as a kickoff to primary season. In that spirit, they invited Republican primary voters from New Hampshire to fill the auditorium. Moderator Kaitlin Collins, presumably, would ask questions that Republican voters cared about. They would then be able to use Trump's answers to gauge whether to vote for him.

That's not what happened.

Instead, Collins asked a series of questions only *Democrats* care about. She asked about Jan. 6. She asked about Trump's election denial. She asked about classified documents. She asked about E. Jean Carroll. In short, Collins provided Trump with precisely what he wanted: an adversarial CNN foe he could absolutely pummel, to the delight of the friendly crowd. The entire event played to Trump's strengths: he was aggressive; he was funny, and transgressively funny at that (of E. Jean Carroll, he noted disbelievingly, "her cat was named Vagina!"); and he refused to give an inch on any of his positions.

Trump under fire from the Left draws nothing but admiration from most Republicans, who constantly feel that they are scurrilously attacked but rarely see a defender willing to go dirty to defend them. Trump defending himself deploys the methodologies they wish Republican politicians would use to defend them. And so, CNN boosted Trump.

CNN found itself on the wrong end of the outrage machine from the liberal commentariat. The irrepressibly insipid Rep. Alexandria Ocasio-Cortez, D-NY., tweeted, "CNN should be ashamed of themselves ... Everyone here saw exactly what was going to happen." MSNBC's Joe Scarborough likened the event to Jan. 6. The Daily Beast's Justin Baragona related that a CNN on-air personality couldn't stop lamenting the "Trump infomercial."

But was the event bad for CNN? Not really. As Trump—who always says the quiet part out loud, for good and ill—stated, CNN brought in the ratings. What's more, CNN *wants Trump to be the nominee,* for both fiscal and political reasons. Trump does indeed mean eyeballs, and eyeballs mean cash. And coincidentally, top Democrats want Trump to be the nominee; President Joe Biden tweeted minutes after the town hall, "It's simple, folks. Do you want four more years of that?"

For now, Trump is the clear front-runner among the Republican candidates. Perhaps his star will dim as he focuses consistently on his own personal Festivus grievances. Or perhaps the media will continue to boost him, providing him with just the adversarial opposition he needs in order to appeal to his base. If the past is any guide, the latter seems far more likely. And then we'll find out whether the Republican base, which apparently believes in Trump's electoral invulnerability despite the elections of 2018 and 2020, is correct—or whether the Democratic base and the media, who apparently believe Trump can't possibly win despite the election of 2016, are mistaken.

The Worst Political Scandal in American History?

May 17, 2023

This week, Special Counsel John Durham released a 316-page report detailing the origins of Operation Crossfire Hurricane—the FBI's investigation into supposed connections between the Trump campaign and the Russian government. The report is an astounding expose of corruption and collusion—not between Trump and Russia, but between the Hillary Clinton campaign, friendlies at the FBI and top officials at the Obama administration. As it turns out, Crossfire Hurricane was initiated based on sheer conjecture. That conjecture was trafficked by Hillary's 2016 campaign. And that conjecture served as the basis for a four-year-long witch hunt into a bevy of allegations that ultimately came to nothing.

The story began, Durham reports, in late July 2016, when Australia provided information to the U.S. embassy in London surrounding conversations between Australian diplomats and low-level Trump foreign policy adviser George Papadopoulos, in which Papadopoulos had allegedly suggested that the "Trump team had received some kind of suggestion from Russia that it could assist" in the process of releasing information about Hillary Clinton. This information alone was utilized as the predicate for launching the full-blown Trump-Russia investigation within three days after receipt of the flimsy information. Top FBI officials greenlit the investigation, including Peter Strzok, deputy assistant director of counterintelligence and devoted Trump-hater. The investigation, Durham notes, was launched "before any dialogue with Australia or the Intelligence Community, and prior to any critical analysis of the information itself."

What could have prompted this eagerness? The FBI, as Durham

acknowledges, was already in possession of the so-called Steele Dossier, a compendium of lies and innuendo created by Fusion GPS at the behest of the Clinton campaign. The FBI had also been approached by a second source working with Fusion GPS in July 2016. There appears to have been a push for an investigation prompted by the desires of the Clinton campaign and the perceived necessity of stopping Trump. The FBI's Assistant Legal Attache in London knew the Papadopoulos information was thin but told the Office of the Inspector General that FBI management was "pushing the matter so hard that 'there was no stopping the train,'" making it his job to "grease the skids."

Meanwhile, in July 2016, U.S. intelligence agencies found out about Russian intelligence suggesting that Hillary had approved a campaign plan to gin up allegations of Trump-Russia collusion. On Aug. 3, CIA Director John Brennan "met with the President, Vice President and other senior Administration officials, including but not limited to the Attorney General (who participated remotely) and the FBI Director" and briefed them on the so-called Clinton Plan. Nobody decided to put a hold on the Trump-Russia investigation, despite the relevant fact that all involved now knew of allegations that the entire situation had been drummed up by the Clinton campaign.

And so, in short, we now know that top officials at the White House and the FBI were aware of Hillary Clinton's plan to disseminate information falsely claiming Trump-Russia collusion; the FBI knew full well that the intelligence it had making such accusations was flimsy at best; they all went ahead anyway. For the rest of the election cycle and much of Trump's presidency, the Democrats, media and intelligence community continued to parrot the Trump-Russia collusion lie.

This collusion is significantly worse than Watergate. It involves the former secretary of state and Democratic candidate for president laundering false intelligence information to the FBI; and the FBI, overseen by the candidate's political allies in the Obama administration, using that information as the predicate to open a full-scale investigation *knowing full well that the Clinton campaign could well be behind the allegations in the first place.*

This is patently insane. It destroys any semblance of legitimacy in the FBI. It implicates former President Barack Obama, President Joe Biden, James Clapper, John Brennan and a bevy of other high officials in weaponization of the government to stop Donald Trump. The Russia hoax was much more than a hoax, it turns out. It was a nefarious plan, enacted at the highest levels of government, to corrupt an election and undermine a presidency.

Will Elon Musk Break the Legacy Media Stranglehold?

May 24, 2023

This week, Florida Gov. Ron DeSantis decided to announce his 2024 presidential candidacy on Twitter Spaces, the newest feature on Elon Musk's Twitter. Musk himself would be co-hosting the event, giving DeSantis access to Musk's 141 million Twitter followers. Only after the Twitter launch will DeSantis begin the more typical campaigning, embarking on a series of campaign events across the nation.

DeSantis' decision represents yet another blow to the power of the legacy media. Legacy media outlets have been fighting mad that DeSantis sees no purpose in granting them long-form interviews; while he's happy to answer their questions—and to aggressively confront them—at press conferences, he simply does not trust that legacy media will ask decent questions or edit him fairly. Instead, DeSantis has merely ignored them.

That strategy has resulted in extraordinary hew and cry from our supposed journalistic establishment. This week, Tara Palmeri, senior political correspondent for Puck News, for example, attempted to confront DeSantis with a series of obtuse questions. "I am also Italian American like you," she said, "if that makes any difference to you at all. Why are you against Disney characters? Which one is your favorite one?" When DeSantis declined to engage, she then called him a "paper tiger—a superficially perfect test-tube Republican candidate who, on closer inspection, is probably not ready for prime time."

But perhaps prime time is entirely the problem. After all, it is prime-time television that made glitz and glamour the center of our presidential politics, gave Donald Trump billions of dollars in free media coverage in 2016, then proceeded to label Trump a threat to the republic and a probable Russian asset. It was prime-time television that elevated lies about COVID-19, turning DeSantis into the Enemy of the People while championing disgraced former New York Gov. Andrew Cuomo as a hero; that endlessly trumpeted the false narrative that black Americans are at dire daily threat from police, resulting in billions of dollars of damage from race riots; that ceaselessly promotes the notion that boys can be girls and vice versa.

The same legacy media that pushed those lies now pushes a bottomless well of lies about DeSantis as well: that his wife Casey is like Lady Macbeth; that Florida has banned gay Americans by passing a "Don't Say Gay" bill that, in reality, merely prevents the sexual indoctrination of children; that black Americans are at existential threat in the state; that books are being banned at scale.

Why, precisely, *should* a politician like DeSantis trust them?

He doesn't. And now, thanks to the open forum provided by Musk, he doesn't need to use them to promote his candidacy. He can simply go directly to the people. This is merely an extension of the strategy Donald Trump used so successfully in 2016 when his Twitter account became the most magnetic media property on the planet—only now Trump has relegated himself to Truth Social, even after Musk reinstated his Twitter account.

In any case, the legacy media—instead of re-examining their own biases and asking just why candidates of the Right refuse to appear on their air—have decided to target Musk and Twitter. They suggest that Musk is the newest threat to the republic—after all, if he weren't, would DeSantis be using Twitter for his launch?

Conservatives no longer need the approval of reporters at The New York Times. They no longer need to suffer the indignities of skewed grilling at the hands of partisan hacks who work for the alphabet networks. Times have changed. And DeSantis' Twitter launch is just the latest evidence.

The Dangerous Trump Indictment

June 14, 2023

This week, a Rubicon was crossed: The former president of the United States and current Republican front-runner for the presidential nomination, Donald Trump, was indicted on 37 federal felony charges relating to mishandling classified information and obstruction of justice. Needless to say, this has never happened before—and the precedent is horrifying. Trump himself campaigned in 2016 promising to "lock up" Hillary Clinton, but he certainly made no moves toward doing so once he entered the White House. But now, President Joe Biden's Department of Justice has done just that. And *that* means that, turnabout being fair play, future elections will carry the risk that the loser may find him or herself in the dock in retaliation.

The choice to indict Trump is particularly egregious given the fact that in 2016, Clinton *wasn't* prosecuted for similar activity. Clinton, it should be remembered, held tens of thousands of emails on a private server, dozens of which were classified; James Comey, then head of the FBI admitted that there was a good shot that foreign sources could have accessed that server; the emails themselves were then destroyed by Clinton's team, and her hard drive cleansed; nonetheless, months later, copies of those emails showed up on the laptop of moral derelict Anthony Weiner. Suffice it to say, Hillary undoubtedly engaged in both gross negligence in handling classified information and obstruction of justice. But Comey declined to prosecute, rewriting the law in order to reach that decision.

And then there is the Biden family. Allegations surrounding corruption within the Biden family continue to abound—and yet law enforcement seems peculiarly unconcerned with such allegations. According to Republican Congress members, a whistleblower has now revealed that the Biden family received millions of dollars in exchange for favors done while Joe Biden was vice president. And yet Biden continues to receive not only the benefit of the doubt, but sycophantic treatment in the press.

Americans remember the Hillary precedent and the Biden apathy as they see Trump in the dock this week. Trump certainly does.

Now, two things can be true at once: the allegations against Trump in the federal indictment are damning, if proved true. The indictment alleges not just that Trump took home classified documents—something done by public figures ranging from Joe Biden to Mike Pence to Hillary Clinton—but that he proceeded to tell his lawyers to attest that he had turned those documents back in, all the while shifting the documents themselves around to avoid his own lawyers knowing about them; that he bragged to journalists about classified documents in his possession while acknowledging that he had not in fact declassified them; that those documents did contain highly important national security information. Had Hillary been indicted in 2016, there would be little doubt about Trump's indictment.

But she wasn't. Which means that our justice system seems to be following the famous Latin American saying: "For my friends, everything; for my enemies, the law." And that double standard will not hold. Which, presumably, is why Trump is already pledging to prosecute the Biden family should he be reelected.

We've entered an ugly new phase in American political history. Trump should have known that his enemies were after him; only epic narcissism and foolishness can explain his behavior in relation to the boxes of documents that have now landed him in court. But such concerns are now secondary. The real question is whether one set of rules will ever again be applied by federal law enforcement— or whether the cycle of tit-for-tat will now enter into full force.

Joe Biden, Hunter Biden, And Parental 'Love'

June 28, 2023

This week, Republicans in the House of Representatives revealed the testimony of an IRS whistleblower who worked on the Hunter Biden investigation. That whistleblower had two revelations to present. First, he said that the federal prosecutor overseeing Hunter's case told at least six witnesses that he had been blocked by Attorney General Merrick Garland from special counsel status—status that would allow him a free hand in fully investigating Hunter. Second, the whistleblower presented a WhatsApp message between Hunter Biden and a Chinese executive shaking down the executive for cash by leveraging Joe Biden's *presence in the room.*

"I am sitting here with my father," Hunter texted, "and we would like to understand why the commitment made has not been fulfilled. Tell the director that I would like to resolve this now before it gets out of hand, and now means tonight. And, Z, if I get a call or text from anyone involved in this other than you, Zhang, or the chairman, I will make certain that between the man sitting next to me and every person he knows and my ability to forever hold a grudge that you will regret not following my direction. I am sitting here waiting for the call with my father."

This was not the first piece of evidence clearly linking Joe to Hunter's influence-peddling operation. Hunter's laptop infamously contained a message from one of Hunter's business partners, James Gilliar, suggesting that 10% of a deal with CEFC China Energy Co. be "held by H for the big guy." Gilliar, in other texts, has also referred to Joe Biden as "the big guy." And Hunter himself complained in text messages to his daughter, Naomi, "I hope you all can do what I did and pay for everything for this entire family for 30 years. It's really hard. But don't worry, unlike pop, I won't make you give me half your salary."

Joe Biden, for the little it's worth, has claimed to know nothing about Hunter's business activities. That's absolutely uncredible, considering that Joe squired Hunter around on Air Force Two, including to China—where Hunter signed lucrative deals—and that Hunter's business partner Tony Bobulinksi alleges he met personally with Joe Biden over business issues.

The credulous reaction to this obvious trail of corruption from many in the media has been incredible to behold. The going line these days in Biden-allied media is that Joe's suspected influence-peddling operation and pressure on his Attorney General to dump the Hunter investigation isn't corruption—it's *actually* a sign of his magnificent parental love. In the words of The New York Times' Nicholas Kristof, "The real meaning of the Hunter Biden saga, as I see it, isn't about presidential corruption, but is about how widespread addiction is—and about how a determined parent with unconditional love can sometimes reel a child back ... That can give others hope."

Meanwhile, this loving father isn't exactly a loving grandfather when it comes to Hunter's illegitimate child, Navy Joan. The same week Hunter was let off the hook by Biden's Department of Justice, Biden signed a child support agreement with former stripper Lunden Roberts in which Roberts accepted a deal including a massive reduction in child support *and* a prohibition on Navy Joan using the Biden family name. Joe himself refuses to acknowledge the existence of Navy Joan. Yes, that famed Biden name is apparently reserved for raising cash in Ukraine and China; those who are actually sired by Hunter Biden in untoward circumstances are disowned by the upstanding Biden family.

Joe surely loves Hunter. But that love is twisted. Hunter is a 53-year-old wreck of a human being with a trail of abuses of other human beings behind him. Joe may have helped curb Hunter's addiction, but he has also apparently used his son as a tool and continues to use him as a crutch—and meanwhile, Joe has enabled Hunter throughout his adult life, humoring his egregiously evil behavior. The story here, then, is twofold: political corruption, and the corruption of familial love into something much uglier.

The Highly Dangerous Georgia Indictments

August 16, 2023

This week, Fulton County District Attorney Fani Willis launched a 98-page missile directly into the heart of American politics. That missile was a 41-count indictment charging former President Donald Trump and 18 alleged co-conspirators with violation of the Georgia version of the Racketeering Influenced and Corrupt Organizations Act—acts in furtherance of a conspiracy to commit a criminal act. In this case, the criminal act, according to the indictment, was "knowingly and willfully (joining) a conspiracy to unlawfully change the outcome of the election in favor of Trump."

Whether this amounts to a crime comes down to the question of whether Trump himself knew that he had lost the election; if he believed that he had won, then all the other accusations about him fall away. After all, it is not a crime to pursue a spurious legal strategy in furtherance of a delusion. But by charging RICO, Willis extends the case to people who may have admitted that Trump lost the election. This accomplishes two purposes. First, it puts these alleged co-conspirators in serious legal jeopardy, giving them reason to flip on Trump himself. Second, it may allow Willis to charge Trump as part of a criminal conspiracy *even if* he personally believed he won the election—after all, case law suggests that co-conspirators can be charged under RICO even if they didn't agree on every aspect of the conspiracy, so long as they knew the "general nature of the enterprise."

The Georgia case also presents unique danger to Trump because it is a *state case.* The Manhattan case against Trump rooted in campaign finance allegations is incredibly weak and is an obvious stretch; the Florida and D.C. cases against Trump are federal, which means that if elected president, he could theoretically pardon himself. The Georgia case is both wide-ranging and state-based: if convicted, Trump would go to state prison, and would have no ability to pardon himself. Georgia Gov. Brian Kemp does not have unilateral pardon power, either: In Georgia, pardons work through an appointed board. So, the very real prospect exists that even were Trump elected, he'd start his term from a state prison.

But even that discussion is premature: The Georgia case, along with all the other indictments against Trump, are going to lock him into courthouses for the rest of the election cycle. What's more, every waking moment for the media will be coverage of those court cases. That will make it impossible for Trump—even if he were so inclined, which has shown no evidence of being—to talk about President Joe Biden rather than his legal peril. And there has yet to be a single piece of data suggesting that Americans are driven to vote for Trump because of his legal troubles. To pardon yourself, you have to be elected president. But spending your entire presidential race in the dock makes that a radically uphill battle.

All of this is quite terrible for the country. No matter what you think of Trump's various legal imbroglios—from mishandling classified documents to paying off porn stars to calling up the Georgia secretary of state in an attempt to "find" votes—the glass has now been broken over and over and over again: Political opponents can be targeted by legal enemies. It will not be unbroken. If you think that only Democratic district attorneys will play this game, you have another thing coming. Prepare for a future in which running for office carries the legal risk of going to jail—on all sides. Which means that only the worst and the most shameless will run for office.

Joe Biden Is a Narcissist, Not an Empath

August 23, 2023

President Joe Biden, we keep hearing, is a deeply empathetic man. It is that empathy that brought him to the presidency—his deep and abiding capacity to connect with others. In "What It Takes," Richard Ben Cramer's detailed blow-by-blow of the 1988 election cycle, Ben Cramer describes Biden's ability to "connect" as his greatest supposed skill. This has been the pitch for Biden for decades: not much in the way of brains, not a tremendously resourceful politician, awkward on his feet—but he *cares.* In the words of Mark Gitenstein, Biden's 1988 speechwriter and a four-decade adviser, "His ability to communicate with people in pain is maybe his most powerful strength."

Or maybe, just maybe, Biden was never an empathetic man. Maybe he simply trafficked in ersatz empathy, all the while feeding his own narcissism.

That story certainly looks more plausible these days.

This week, Biden visited Maui. He did so nearly two weeks after the worst wildfire in modern American history killed hundreds of Americans. Meanwhile, Biden vacationed in Delaware on the beach, telling reporters he had "no comment" on the situation; he then jet-set off to Lake Tahoe before finally heading to Lahaina. Once he reached Hawaii, he proceeded to explain that he felt the pain of those whose family members had been incinerated. After all, he said, one time he experienced a small kitchen fire. "I don't want to compare difficulties, but we have a little sense, Jill and I, of what it was like to lose a home," he jabbered. "Years ago, now, 15 years, I was in Washington doing 'Meet the press' … Lightning struck at home on a little lake outside the home, not a lake a big pond. It hit the wire and came up underneath our home, into the … air condition ducts. To make a long story short, I almost lost my wife, my '67 Corvette and my cat."

In reality, back in 2004, lightning caused a kitchen fire in Biden's home that was put out in 20 minutes with no other damage.

If this were an isolated incident, we could chalk it up to Biden's encroaching senility. But it isn't. After presiding over the botched pullout from Afghanistan that resulted in the return of the Taliban, the murder of 13 American servicemembers, the abandonment of hundreds of American citizens and thousands of American green card holders, and the subjugation of some tens of millions of women, Biden essentially shrugged. Then, when faced with the families of wounded and killed American soldiers, he attempted to "feel their pain" by invoking the death of his son, Beau. According to Cheryl Rex, whose son died in the Abbey Gate bombing of Aug. 26, 2021, "His words to me were, 'My wife, Jill, and I know how you feel. We lost our son as well and brought him home in a flag-draped coffin.'"

Biden has cited Beau in similar instances multiple times.

In the Jewish community, death of a loved one is followed by shiva, a seven-day period of mourning. During shiva, mourners don't leave their homes; they are instead cared for by the community, provided with food and communal prayer. Members of the community visit the shiva house to provide comfort.

The first rule of visiting a shiva house: Don't talk about your own experiences with death or pain. It's gauche and irrelevant and trivializing.

Yet this is Biden's first move.

Empathy is the quality of putting yourself in the place of others. But Biden isn't an empath. He's someone who believes that everyone else's pain is merely a reflection of his own.

The Impeachment of Joe Biden

September 13, 2023

This week, House Speaker Kevin McCarthy, R-Calif., announced the opening of an impeachment inquiry into President Joe Biden. "These are allegations of abuse of power, obstruction and corruption, and they warrant further investigation by the House of Representatives," McCarthy explained. The impeachment inquiry will give the House Republicans a better legal defense against claims that any subpoenas they issue exceed the scope of congressional authority. More importantly, it signals to the American public the seriousness of Republican intent to make Biden's corruption the top issue in the 2024 election.

For those complaining about Republican politicking, turnabout is surely fair play. Former President Donald Trump was impeached not once but twice; neither time did Democrats so much as allege a statutory crime. They relied on the fact that impeachment is a political response, not a criminal one—true as far as it goes, but precedent-setting in the context of prior impeachments. They pursued impeachment inquiries without so much as a vote in the House. The genie is out of the bottle, and it isn't going back in anytime soon.

The allegations against Biden are already damning. So is the evidence. Biden used his son, Hunter, as a cutout to clear cash from foreign sources on behalf of the Biden family. That's all part of a decadeslong pattern by which Biden has used his political power and influence to benefit his family. Back in the 1970s, Jimmy Biden, Joe's brother, somehow obtained generous loans from a local bank to open a rock club, despite little in the way of collateral; Joe was sitting on the Senate Banking Committee at the time and ended up pressuring the bank when Jimmy fell behind on his loans. In 1996, Joe cashed out his home by selling it to the vice president of MBNA in a sweetheart deal; MBNA would also hire Hunter fresh out of law school. MBNA was one of Biden's biggest donors and a beneficiary of his credit card policy largesse. In the words of Politico reporter Ben Schreckinger, "The Bidens regularly intermingled personal, political, and financial relationships in ways that invited questions about whether the public interest was getting short-changed."

All of this came to a head when Joe attained the vice presidency. Hunter forged relationships, with his father's aide, in China and Ukraine; Joe would call into business meetings to "talk about the weather." Hunter joined the board of Burisma, where he made an extraordinary amount of money; in return, he promised connection with his father. In December 2015, Biden went to Ukraine, where he demanded that Viktor Shokin, a prosecutor looking into Burisma, be fired, threatening to withdraw $1 billion in American aid. During this time, a confidential human source later told the FBI that Burisma's CFO said that he had hired Hunter "to protect us, through his dad, from all kinds of problems."

That was merely the most egregious apparent abuse of power. There were dozens of others.

Was Joe benefitting from Hunter's business arrangements? We hear from the media that there is no evidence to suggest he was. But that's obviously a lie: scoring benefits for your drug-addicted, sexually deviant son is certainly a benefit that accrues to Joe. And we also have a text directly from Hunter to his daughter Naomi in 2019: "I hope you can all do what I did and pay for everything for this entire family for 30 years. It's really hard. But don't worry. Unlike Pop, I won't make you give me half your salary."

All of this is predicate to Biden's behavior as president. Thanks to whistleblowers, we know that the Biden DOJ attempted to cut a sweetheart deal with Hunter Biden to end any investigation into these matters. In this case, the cover-up may be just as bad as the crime.

In the end, the American voters will give their verdict on Biden; with Democrats in control of the Senate, he won't be removed from office. But Republicans are right to remind Americans that Biden isn't a decent man restoring honor to the Oval Office. He's a career-long corrupt politician who simply got lucky in his enemies at the right time.

Why Trump Is Winning

December 13, 2023

So, according to the legacy media, disaster is about to befall America.

Former President Donald Trump is the overwhelming favorite to win the Republican presidential nomination: The latest Des Moines Register/NBC News poll shows Trump at 51% in Iowa, up 8% since October, with Florida Gov. Ron DeSantis in a distant second at 19% and Nikki Haley at 16%. According to analyst Steve Kornacki, there is an enthusiasm gap in favor of Trump: 70% of Trump supporters say their minds are made up. He is currently at 72% favorability with Iowa caucusgoers.

In the general, Trump is also up. And he's not up by a small margin. He is up significantly.

Donald Trump, if the election were held today, would become president of the United States. According to a Wall Street Journal poll over the weekend, Trump leads President Joe Biden 47% to 43% in the national polls; if third-party and independent candidates enter the mix, that lead jumps to six points, 37% to 31%. What's more, according to the latest CNN poll, Trump leads Biden by 10 points in Michigan; he leads by five in Georgia.

There are two reasons for this.

First, Joe Biden is terribly, terribly unpopular. That same Wall Street Journal poll shows that just 23% of voters say Biden's policies have helped them personally, compared to 53% who say his policies have hurt them. Meanwhile, half of voters say that Trump's policies helped them versus 37% who say they hurt. Biden's job performance is at 37% approval and 61% disapproval; just 30% of voters like Bidenomics.

That condition is unlikely to alleviate for Biden before the election. It is, according to The Wall Street Journal, "less affordable than any time in recent history to buy a home, and the math isn't changing any time soon." Average new home payments currently stand at $3,322, up from $1,746 at the end of 2020. What's more, Biden's supposed soft landing doesn't look particularly likely to happen, despite the happy talk from the media. November job growth was weak—which is what the Fed was looking for when they raised interest rates in order to tamp down inflation. But that job growth was only even in "weak" territory because of health care, government employment and leisure and hospitality. In fact, those three sectors plus private education employment are responsible for 81% of all jobs created in 2023. Business starts are weak. Gross output—a measure of the entire economy, not merely the spending side that we see in gross domestic product—has flatlined. In the first two quarters of the year, business spending dropped 9%.

Biden's team keeps trying to whistle their way past the graveyard on his candidacy. The literal graveyard. According to Semafor's Ben Smith, at the White House holiday party, Biden "strayed into a couple of hazy monologues, which ended only when his wife interrupted him to remind him it was a party. His speech wasn't terrible, or even noteworthy. But everyone in the room realized Biden had a simple rhetorical job and hadn't quite pulled it off."

That's right: Joe Biden literally couldn't get through a holiday speech at the White House.

This brings us to the second reason Trump is leading Biden in the polls right now: he's not in the news. That's also the reason he's up in Iowa head and shoulders above the rest of the candidates. Because he's not in the news, he's beating Biden—that takes the electability argument away from DeSantis and Haley. And because he's not in the news, everyone has been able to look away from Trump's crazy, which has always been his Achilles heel. Ironically, one of the best things ever to happen to Trump politically was his social media ban: it has made him nearly invisible.

So, here's the question: Will things stay this way?

Biden's approval ratings are unlikely to recover from where they are now. The economy is in tender shape. The Ukraine war is going badly. Israel is going to have to continue its war not only against Hamas but against Hezbollah and possibly the Yemeni Houthis.

Which means Biden's only hope is putting Trump front and

center. That could happen via Trump's criminal trials—but that may be largely baked into the Trump cake at this point. Would even a conviction radically shift people's opinions on Trump?

Today's Trump advantage is no mere chimera. It may just be the 2024 reality. Which is why the media and Democrats are panicking, and they should be.

Barring Trump From Ballots Is a Recipe for Violence

December 20, 2023

On Tuesday evening, the Supreme Court of Colorado ruled that former President Donald J. Trump had to be removed from the state ballot, for both the primaries and the general election. They cited Amendment 14, Section 3 of the Constitution of the United States, which states, in relevant part, that candidates are ineligible for office if they "shall have engaged in insurrection or rebellion" against the Constitution of the United States. It is unclear whether the provision applies to presidential candidates; it is even more unclear whether such a provision is "self-enforcing," meaning that any electoral official in any state can simply declare for himself whether a candidate has been an "insurrectionist."

Nonetheless, the court said it is qualified to determine who is guilty of "insurrection" under the 14th Amendment without any criminal case or impeachment case. And the court says that "the events of January 6 constituted an insurrection and... President Trump engaged in that insurrection."

On a legal level, this is extraordinarily strained. Section 3 was designed to prohibit those who had served in the Confederacy from holding public office in the United States. The Confederacy, as we know, was an armed rebellion against the United States that ended in the deaths of some 600,000 Americans on both sides. Trump, by contrast, made a series of legal challenges to the election, all of which were denied, and then claimed—on the basis of specious legal reasoning—that the vice president could simply throw out electoral slates that had already been certified. He then called for his supporters to protest at the Capitol building and a riot broke out. This hardly qualifies as an "insurrection," let alone proving that

Trump engaged in one. Trump, let us not forget, has not been charged with insurrection. He was not even convicted in his impeachment trial over Jan. 6.

Yet the Colorado State Supreme Court says it can bar him from electoral eligibility anyway.

This is, to put it mildly, unbelievably dangerous.

It sets up a perverse set of incentives for both political sides.

Trump can and will rightly claim that lawfare has been used to thwart the workings of democracy—that a slate of judges in any state can simply negate the will of the voters, and that President Joe Biden's own Department of Justice has been attempting to drag him into court before the election in order to stymie his shot at the presidency.

Meanwhile, the Colorado Supreme Court has now set up expectations for Democrats across the country that Trump can be legally barred from the presidency—and when the Supreme Court overturns that Colorado Supreme Court ruling, they will claim that the Supreme Court itself is rigged.

All of which means that 2024 is going to be the most insane and ugly presidential election in American history. And that's saying a lot, since 1968 and 2020 are both years that existed. Under what circumstances, precisely, would Democrats accept the result of a Trump election? Under what circumstances, precisely, would Republicans accept the result of a Biden election?

The weaponization of the legal system creates an all-consuming fire, burning everything in its path. There is simply no 2024 result likely to result in anything but complete—and perhaps violent—chaos at this point.

In 2024, Trump Has the Advantage

January 3, 2024

The 2024 election is coming.

And right now, it's Advantage: Trump.

Former President Donald Trump is leading by 2.2% in the RealClearPolitics polling average. That doesn't sound like a lot until you realize that Trump trailed Joe Biden in that same average on election day 2020 by 7.2%—and only lost by 4.5%. Or that Hillary Clinton was leading in that same average by 3.2% on Election Day 2016—and only won the popular vote by 2.1%. Donald Trump almost always outdraws his polling number.

What's more, Biden is stuck in neutral. Why? The answer is obvious: Biden lied to voters. He campaigned as a moderate in the primaries, capitalized on that image in the general while pushing steadily to the Left, and then governed from the Left. Now, says political scientist Ruy Teixeira, "Biden is polling behind Trump nationally and in every swing state, with the possible exception of Wisconsin. Trump is preferred to Biden by wide margins on voters' most important issue, the economy and inflation, as well as their second most important issue, immigration and border security and on crime and public safety. Biden's approval rating at this point in his presidency is the lowest of any president going back to the 1940s, when the era of modern polling began."

Biden thinks that Trump-bashing will save him.

That's presumably why he's going to go on a Trump-bashing tour beginning this week, labeling Trump a racist and a fascist. According to the Associated Press, "President Joe Biden is starting the campaign year by evoking the Revolutionary War to mark the third anniversary of the deadly insurrection at the U.S. Capitol and visiting the South Carolina church where a white gunman massacred Black parishioners—seeking to present in the starkest possible terms an election he argues could determine the fate of American democracy."

This isn't likely to work. At all.

It's unlikely to work because everyone knows Trump. Everything about Trump is baked into the cake. Everyone knows that Trump's 2020 post-election activities didn't change the outcome of the election—Biden, after all, is president. What's more, the pitch that Trump is more racist than Biden doesn't work. Biden is the DEI president, a man who has yammered incessantly in favor of racial carve-outs and staffed his own administration on the basis of intersectional characteristics.

The pitch that Trump is a fascist won't work either. As even George Will, a Trump opponent, points out, "Joe Biden is, like Trump, an authoritarian recidivist mostly stymied by courts." Will gives a litany of Biden constitutional violations: "the eviction moratorium, the vaccine mandate, the cancellation of student debt," among others.

Most of all, Biden's hope that hatred for Trump will somehow save him is predicated on the idea that heavy turnout against Trump is a foregone conclusion. But ... what if it's not? What if the actual norm is that Trump *doesn't* drive Democratic turnout in the way Biden hopes? In 2016, after all, turnout was within historical norms: 59.2% of eligible voters voted in that year, compared with 58% in 2012 and 60.1% in 2004. In 2020, by contrast, a whopping 66.9% of eligible voters showed up. That last number is a massive outlier. 2020 saw a voter increase of 23 million, to 160 million total voters— as opposed to 137 million in 2016 and 129 million in 2012.

That wasn't because of Trump. It was because of pandemic-era policies that allowed everyone to vote from home months in advance. Do we really think that 2020 turnout number will replicate? If it doesn't, who will those marginal voters come from: Biden or Trump?

This means that Biden is going to have to actually succeed in order to win.

The only thing that might save him would be ... you know, good things happening in America.

But his own policies prevent just that.

Biden's Scare-The-Hell-Out-Of-You Reelection Campaign

January 10, 2024

Joe Biden is facing an uphill reelection battle.

He is desperate, and he should be. The world is an uglier and an uglier place under Biden. Nearly no one believes the country is moving in the right direction. Americans are deeply dissatisfied with the economy; America is experiencing an unprecedented illegal immigration crisis; and the world seems to be on fire, from the Middle East to Ukraine.

Meanwhile, Biden himself is clearly ailing; as comedian Shane Gillis recently said, "My favorite thing about Biden is anytime Biden finishes a speech, he transforms into a Roomba." This is clearly true. In fact, after Biden's recent diatribe against Donald Trump at Valley Forge, Dr. Jill Biden—the greatest physician in all the land—charged up on the stage like a shepherd attempting to pen in a wandering sheep, corralling the president toward the back of the stage.

So, what can Biden do?

He can pull out all the scare tactics he knows.

And that's precisely what he's doing, fully 10 months from the 2024 election.

His campaign is predicated on two main issues: Trump, and also Trump.

First, Biden argues, Donald Trump is apparently a threat to democracy. Biden stated at Valley Forge, "Donald Trump's campaign is obsessed with the past, not the future. He's willing to sacrifice our democracy, put himself in power." He said this in the middle of a speech about the evils of Jan. 6—while labeling Trump an insurrectionist, which presumably would disqualify Trump from the ballot. Biden's own Department of Justice has hit Trump with two separate federal criminal cases, one in Florida, the other in Washington, D.C.

It is, in other words, a tough case to make that Trump is the true threat to democracy, while Biden is democracy's defender.

Second, Biden argues, Donald Trump is a white supremacist. Biden stated at Emanuel AME Church in Charleston, South Carolina—the site of a white supremacist mass shooting in 2015—that Trump's election denial represented a "second lost cause," somehow comparable to the Southern Lost Cause narrative that portrayed the loss of the Civil War as the death of a grand and glorious way of life at the hands of perfidious Yankees. Yes, Biden suggested, Trump was akin to the Confederates. And he, Joe Biden, would stand in their way.

Biden has made this case before. Against—yes, really—Mitt Romney. Back in 2012, Biden argued that Romney would put Black Americans "back in chains." Suffice it to say that Biden has little credibility trying to breathe new life into that political corpse.

Joe Biden requires Donald Trump. He needs him.

But he's still unlikely to beat him.

That's why Biden is steering so strongly to his left rather than toward the middle. At his speech in Charleston, pro-Hamas protesters began chanting for a ceasefire in Gaza, which would leave Hamas in power after the Oct. 7 massacre. Biden sheepishly replied, "I understand their passion, and I've been quietly working with the Israeli government to get them to reduce and significantly get out of Gaza."

Biden can't leave any stone, no matter how radical, unturned.

And that tactic will, in turn, drive away many moderate voters who are sick of the chaos the Biden era has ushered in.

In short, Biden is re-running his 2020 campaign. There's one big difference this time: This time, Joe Biden is the president. And we all know it.

Why Donald Trump Won the GOP Nomination

January 17, 2024

Donald Trump is the presumptive Republican nominee for president after a dominant performance in the Iowa caucuses—a performance in which he earned over 50% of the vote and left his closest competitors in the dust. Trump currently leads in the polls in New Hampshire, South Carolina and every other primary state.

Get ready for "Trump vs. Biden II: Electric Boogaloo."

The big question, of course, is *why?* Why does Trump retain such a grip on the Republican imagination after losing the 2020 election, contributing heavily to the loss of two Republican Senate seats in Georgia in 2021, and contributing heavily to the loss of the Senate in 2022 with his spate of bizarre primary picks? Why should Trump, who spends much of every day fulminating about his upcoming legal cases, have the upper hand against Republicans without such baggage? Why does Trump, who is certainly no conservative ideologue, live so large in the imagination of conservatives?

There are several reasons.

Primarily, Trump is lucky in his enemies.

To be more precise, Trump's very presence on the political stage—and his victory over Hillary Clinton in 2016—drove his enemies out of their minds. Those enemies determined that any and all means were appropriate for undermining his presidency and his 2020 reelection bid: from Russian collusion nonsense to multiple impeachments, from nodding at historically damaging riots to blaming him for a pandemic, from changing the voting rules to lying about and then shutting down the dissemination of the Hunter Biden laptop story, anything was on the table. So when Trump claimed in the post-2020 election landscape that he had been robbed of victory, that contention rang true, even if his contentions about outright voter fraud remained unproven.

Trump has been the title character of "Trump: The Series" since 2015. In the end, the chances that Americans would allow a recasting before his reelection effort were always low. But those chances shrank to zero the moment Trump's enemies weaponized the legal system against him.

When Trump's enemies, in the aftermath of Joe Biden's election win, continued to come after Trump using the legal system, Trump argued that he was a stand-in for conservatives everywhere, who feel that they are targeted for destruction by America's most powerful institutions. That argument had major purchase: by polling data, Trump's bump to the top of the Republican 2024 heap came not with his reelection announcement, but with the announcement in March 2023 that he would be indicted in Manhattan on specious charges of campaign finance violation. The drumbeat of new legal charges against him, dropped everywhere from Florida to Washington, D.C. to Georgia, simply added fuel to the fire.

Perhaps even that legal news could have been turned against Trump in a primary race. But there was one more factor Trump needed: He needed Joe Biden to be so terrible at his job, so outright awful, that Trump would suddenly look competitive. The electability argument—the argument that Trump's losing record since 2016 would continue into 2024—collapsed for Trump's Republican opponents as Biden's approval rating sank into the 30s. Republicans' hearts were with Trump; now their heads could be with him, too.

And so Trump is the presumptive nominee.

The only question is whether he will reenter the White House in January 2025. And that question, ironically, will be answered less by Trump than by Biden. Trump's campaign will be relatively quiet: He'll be relegated to courtrooms and TruthSocial; there will be no debates. Which means that 2024 could easily be a referendum on Biden's presidency. And if that happens, Trump will have capped the most remarkable political comeback since Richard Nixon won the White House in 1968.

Will Biden's Age Finish His Campaign?

February 14, 2024

Last week, Joe Biden's presidential reelection campaign fell apart.

To be fair, it's been a long time coming: Biden himself is deeply unpopular by every polling metric, running behind his chief Republican rival, Donald Trump, on nearly every major issue. With the world on fire—war in Ukraine, a conflagration in Gaza, shipping harassed in the Red Sea, the ongoing threat of Chinese intervention against Taiwan—and a widespread feeling of domestic economic instability based on continued higher-than-expected inflation, with an open border promoted by the White House and culture wars dividing the nation, Biden's reelection prospects were already weak.

And then, the special counsel in Biden's classified documents case proceeded to tell the truth about Biden's mental health status.

And all hell broke loose.

The special counsel report makes clear that Biden obviously violated the law. According to the special counsel, Biden "willfully retained and disclosed classified materials after his vice presidency when he was a private citizen." But, the special counsel concluded, Biden is simply too old and feeble to prosecute: "We have also considered that, at trial, Mr. Biden would likely present himself to a jury, as he did during our interview of him, as a sympathetic, well-meaning, elderly man with a poor memory."

According to the special counsel, Biden's memory failures were repeated and troubling: "He did not remember when he was vice president, forgetting on the first day of the interview when his term ended ('if it was 2013—when did I stop being Vice President?'), and forgetting on the second day of the interview when his term began ('in 2009, am I still Vice President?'). He did not remember, even within several years, when his son Beau died. And his memory appeared hazy when describing the Afghanistan debate that was once so important to him."

Biden knew that he had to fight back against the perception that he is decrepit. And so he called a press conference. And at that press conference, he proceeded to light himself on fire. First, he tried to claim that questioning his memory regarding his son's death was somehow unkind or nasty; next, he forgot where that same son had obtained his rosary; finally, he mixed up the president of Egypt and the president of Mexico. Then he stumbled into the wings.

And suddenly, Biden's age issues were apparent for all to see. They were, in fact, inescapable. An ABC News/Ipsos poll in the aftermath of the press conference showed that 86% of Americans believe Biden is too old to serve another term as president. To put that in context, by some polling data, only 80% of Americans agree that the earth is round; just 71% agree that NASA landed on the moon. Essentially, only members of Biden's paid staff and his immediate family believe he is capable of serving another term.

Which means that Biden is in trouble.

All Donald Trump has to do to defeat him is to shut up.

And herein lies the problem. Trump's tendency to put himself in the headlines overlaps perfectly with the media's desire to put him front and center in the campaign, rather than Biden's political and mental incompetence. Trump loves the rallies; he loves the lights. In reality, he'd be best off running Biden's 2020 basement strategy, allowing Biden himself to be the issue of the election.

Will Trump do that? History suggests he won't. Which means that we're in for a nail-biter of a race—and an unprecedently chaotic, messy and incoherent campaign.

The Dirty Little Secret of the 2024 Campaign

March 6, 2024

This week, new polling showed what Democrats have long feared: Donald Trump is now in commanding position to defeat Joe Biden and win reelection in 2024. According to the latest New York Times/Siena poll, Trump is up 48-43 over Biden; what's more, Biden is actually underwater among Hispanics, earns just two-thirds of Black votes, and has cratered among independents. According to the RealClearPolitics polling average, Trump now leads in every swing state but Pennsylvania and is within the margin of error there, too. Nationally, Trump has not trailed Biden since September 2023.

We all know what's going wrong for Biden: He's widely perceived as too old to be running again; Americans remain unhappy with the economy, deeply enraged over border policy and alarmed by the brush fires around the world. Biden came into office promising normalcy, and he has instead delivered chaos.

But there's something else going on, too.

Joe Biden is losing to Donald Trump because of a dirty little secret: Donald Trump is actually the moderate in this race.

On nearly every issue, Trump is closer to the median voter than Biden. Biden won the Democratic primaries over Sen. Bernie Sanders in 2020 because voters thought he would tack toward the center, away from the insanity of The Squad in Congress— borderline psychotics like Reps. Cori Bush, Alexandria Ocasio-Cortez, Rashida Tlaib and Ilhan Omar. Instead, he entered office believing that he had a mandate for transformation, that he could become our age's FDR or LBJ.

And so Biden abandoned the middle.

And median voters are now abandoning Biden. As election

analyst Nate Silver rightly observes, The New York Times poll shows that "only 83 percent of voters who say they chose Biden in 2020 plan to vote for him this year, whereas 97 percent who voted for Trump plan to vote for Trump again. These are swing voters, in other words—people who are explicitly stating to pollsters that they are switching their vote from 2020. There are a substantial number of them." Because the legacy media are monolithically radical on matters of politics, they keep encouraging Biden to double down on the left-wing base, hoping that by steering toward the radicals, he can boost voter turnout. But that strategy is leaving independent voters behind.

Meanwhile, Trump is winning over more and more vote-switchers. That's because his positions are *moderate.* On abortion, for example, he may support a federal 16-week ban. By polling data, 48% of Americans support such a ban, compared with 36% who oppose such a ban. Only 24% of Americans support Biden's position—availability of abortion without limits. On immigration, Biden is underwater by over 20 points. On inflation and spending, Americans favor lower inflation and lower spending—both propositions that cut against Biden's preferred policies. On national security, Americans broadly favor Israel over Hamas—and yet Biden's administration has steered toward the pro-Hamas voters in Dearborn, Michigan.

For some reason, Biden and his team think that their echo chamber strategy—shouting "Jan. 6!" over and over while demonizing their political opposition as insurrectionists and traitors—is likely to jog enough base turnout to overcome their loss of the middle. But that's a chimerical proposition. Biden, in other words, has been suckered by the very people who want him to win most—the radicals in the media who keep ramming him toward the far left, even as he falls further and further behind in the polling.

Why I'm Co-Hosting a Trump Fundraiser

March 20, 2024

Unsurprisingly to those who follow this space, I plan to vote for Donald Trump in November. Not just that. This week, I'm co-hosting a fundraiser for him.

So, how precisely did a conservative who didn't vote for president in 2016 and didn't support Donald Trump during the Republican primaries become a Trump donor? The answer is obvious: Donald Trump's opponent is Joe Biden. And Joe Biden is the worst president of my lifetime.

Because Donald Trump is the nominee against Joe Biden, I won't just vote for him. I'll go into my own pocket to support him. Which is what I'm doing.

My calculus is simple: America was better off under Donald Trump than it is in under Joe Biden.

At home, America was safer and more prosperous. When Donald Trump was president, we did not have an open border. We were not flooding our country with at least 7 million illegal immigrants, overwhelming our cities, leaving our country wide open to the plague of Chinese- and Mexican drug cartel-backed fentanyl poisoning.

When Donald Trump was president, we did not have a president who tried to use the Occupational Safety and Health Administration to force 80 million Americans to take a vaccine or lose their jobs—and my company didn't have to sue to stop it.

When Donald Trump was president, we did not have 40-year highs in inflation and decreasing real wages.

When Donald Trump was president, we did not have a federal attempt to teach children that boys can be girls and vice versa, or to force taxpayers to subsidize abortion, or to target religious institutions for the great crime of upholding traditional Judeo-Christian values.

When Donald Trump was president, we did not have an administration hell-bent on stymying the police in their attempts to fight crime, or an administration that values diversity and inclusion and wokeness above military readiness, all in the name of "equity."

When Donald Trump was president, we did not have American businesses preparing to have their incomes robbed from them in the name of the biggest spending programs in American history.

When Donald Trump was president, we did not have unconstitutional attempts to simply wipe away student loan debt, or a Department of Justice dedicated to the targeting of political opposition.

When Donald Trump was president, the world was not on fire.

When Donald Trump was president, we did not cut and run in the face of 8th-century barbarians in Afghanistan, who blew up 13 American soldiers, hunted down our allies, and reestablished al-Qaida bases.

When Donald Trump was president, peace was breaking out in the Middle East between Arab nations and Israel, and Iran was in a box. We certainly didn't have a multi-front hot war between Iranian proxies and American allies—or American soldiers directly—and we weren't trying to pay billions in bribes to the Iranian mullahs.

When Donald Trump was president, we didn't have war in Ukraine.

When Donald Trump was president, we didn't have China threatening imminent blockade of Taiwan.

When Donald Trump was president, America was better off.

I'll always be honest with you about Donald Trump. He wasn't my first choice in the primaries; he's a deeply flawed man. I've been open in my criticisms of Trump on both character and policy. And I'm not going to stop criticizing Donald Trump when I disagree with him. I always have, and I always will. That's my job, and the job of all Americans.

But Donald Trump is the man standing between America and a second Joe Biden term. And a second Joe Biden term means America in dire, dire trouble.

It's that simple.

It's Trump or Biden.

Unlike in 2016, we don't have to guess at what a Trump administration will be. And we don't have to guess what a Biden administration will be either. We know. America cannot afford another Joe Biden term.

Or, perhaps more realistically, a Kamala Harris term.

Joe Biden is here to finish the job that Barack Obama started, of fundamentally transforming America into the image of the left. That cannot happen. That's why I'm not just giving Donald Trump my vote, I'm giving him my money. Because this election matters. And Donald Trump must be the next president of the United States.

Joe Biden Is Scared of His Own Shadow

April 17, 2024

This week, the Islamic Republic of Iran—a radical Shariah theocracy hell-bent on the destruction of Israel and Saudi Arabia, among others—fired some 300 drones and missiles at the State of Israel. This is, definitionally, an act of war. Iran claimed that it had attacked Israel in response to Israel's killing of Iranian Revolutionary Guard Corps terror master Gen. Mohammad Reza Zahedi in Syria. In reality, this was merely the latest escalation by Iran, after decades of using its proxies in the Middle East to attack Americans, Israelis and Western allies.

Why, though, did Iran think it could get away with such a launch without serious repercussions—particularly since America directly intervened, along with the U.K., France, Jordan and Saudi Arabia in taking down Iranian ordnance?

The answer is simple: Iran has successfully deterred the United States.

Deterrence, according to the Defense Department, is "the prevention of action by the existence of a credible threat of unacceptable counteraction and/or belief that the cost of action outweighs the perceived benefits." Clearly, the United States has not deterred Iran. Far from it: according to a report from the Jerusalem Post, Iran notified the United States in advance of its barrage against Israel, hoping to attain some sort of assurance that the United States would not retaliate and would pressure Israel to not retaliate, either. According to a Turkish go-between, "Iran informed us in advance of what would happen. Possible developments also came up during the meeting with (Secretary of State Antony) Blinken, and they (the U.S.) conveyed to Iran through us that this reaction must be within certain limits."

This is perfectly repulsive. In short, Iran wanted to engage in a show of strength; they then notified America that they would be attacking an American ally directly in the largest Middle Eastern cross-border attack by a sovereign country on another sovereign country since the Gulf War. And Biden said, "Sure, OK, so long as you don't go too far."

Biden then performed his part: he pressured Israel to "take the win" and not retaliate. After all, Biden said, it wouldn't look good to "escalate" in the region.

Now, the reality is that the best way to deescalate in foreign policy is often to engage in *actual deterrence*. That's why President Donald Trump's approach, mocked by the pseudo-intellectual class, was effective: yes, it was bizarre to watch the sitting president of the United States threaten other world leaders with his "nuclear button," which Trump assured those leaders was "much bigger and more powerful." Also, would *you* want to provoke a man who tweeted such things if you were Kim Jong Un or the ayatollahs?

But Joe Biden doesn't understand deterrence. In fact, *he* is deterred: Iran has successfully launched a war against Israel, and the United States is not only backing down but also pushing Israel to do the same.

So, why is Biden backing down?

Two reasons. First, Biden believes that his reelection effort requires the Middle East to calm. Second, Biden believes that his reelection effort requires the support for pro-Hamas radicals in Michigan. Biden is wrong on both counts, of course: It turns out that appeasement heightens the possibility of conflict in the Middle East, and Biden's attempts to feed the pro-Hamas alligator one bite at a time will eventually end with his candidacy on the plate.

Whatever the rationale, however, the image of the United States under Joe Biden is one of unending cowardice. The Taliban called Biden's bluff; Russia has called Biden's bluff; Iran has called Biden's bluff; how long will it be until China does? Deterrence requires, above all else, willpower. And that is in short supply from a White House that sees strength as a weakness.

Joe Biden, Political Pinwheel

May 15, 2024

Joe Biden is not a person of principle or character. He is a lifelong politician who has spent decades shifting his positions on nearly every major issue. If one had to define Biden's political worldview, it would be simply this: Follow the Democratic herd, and desperately attempt to place yourself dead center in the middle of it. Joe Biden is, in short, a political pinwheel, taking note of the prevailing winds in his own party and seeking to channel them in his favor.

This strategy made Biden a career also-ran. After all, who wants to follow a follower? Biden never achieved any level of national popularity on his own: His presidential runs imploded in embarrassing fashion in 1988 and 2008. His saving grace was, in fact, his blandness and inoffensiveness: Thanks to those peculiarly counterintuitive qualities, Barack Obama made him his vice president. There, Biden thrived as a vice president who presided over little actual policy but happily floated trial balloons for the administration and acted as a rah-rah cheerleader for his more popular boss.

Obama himself had so little faith in his vice president that he passed him over in 2016 in favor of the widely reviled Hillary Clinton. After Clinton lost, Biden threw his hat in the ring—and thanks to the extraordinary incompetence of some of his opponents (Kamala Harris and Amy Klobuchar), the extraordinary dilettantism of others (Pete Buttigieg and Michael Bloomberg), and the befuddled racialism of still others (Bernie Sanders and Elizabeth Warren)—he prevailed by simply fulfilling two conditions: First, he was alive (barely); second, he wasn't any of the other clods.

So Joe Biden became president.

He posed as a political moderate. But there is a difference

between principled moderation and simply bobbing, corklike, about the eddies of internal Democratic politics. Moderation sometimes requires a Sister Souljah moment—a moment when you push away the radicals and embrace the mainstream. Acting as a political pinwheel encourages no such strength. In fact, it encourages the opposite: caving to every interest, at all times.

And thus, Joe Biden has tried to be everything to everyone—and has ended up as no one to anyone. Biden has zero passionate fans, because his positions are all ersatz; he barely even has passionate enemies, since so few of his opponents believe that *he* believes anything he says in the moment. His constant waffling has earned him little loyalty and no victories of note (and no, spending trillions of dollars on wasteful boondoggles isn't a victory; it's just the way government is now done).

Biden's waffling has cost Americans dearly. Stuck between a Modern Monetary Theory left and more fiscally moderate liberals, Biden has halved the baby, opting for big spending and interest rate increases. Trapped between a post-American left and traditionally interventionist Wilsonian liberals, Biden has hedged between militaristic support for Ukraine and slow-walking aid. Caught between an Israel-hating left and Israel-supportive liberals, Biden has declared his support for Israel in its goals of extirpating Hamas and then pressured Israel to leave Hamas in place by promoting Hamas propaganda and embargoing critical weaponry.

It turns out that the presidency is a bad place for pinwheels. The closest thing to a pinwheel president we've had over the past few decades was Bill Clinton—but even Clinton knew to pursue a course once the course had been charted. Biden flips radically between positions—even from day to day—leaving the rest of the world confused and discombobulated.

Americans don't like it. In fact, they don't like it so much that polls show that Joe Biden would be a one-term president if the election were held today—and that he would lose to the man he declares a threat to democracy. Why? Because there is one character aspect on which Donald Trump outpolls Biden by leaps and bounds: leadership. As it turns out, there's no substitute for leadership.

And Joe Biden has never been a leader.

The Campaign of Delusion

May 29, 2024

Here are a few signs of a losing campaign:

No. 1: Poll denial.

No. 2: Inability to shift course.

No. 3: Celebrity cameos.

Welcome to Joe Biden's 2024 campaign.

The Biden campaign is rife with simultaneous panic and poll denial. According to Politico, "A pervasive sense of fear has settled in at the highest levels of the Democratic Party … anxiety has morphed into palpable trepidation, according to more than a dozen party leaders and operatives." Meanwhile, according to Axios, "President Biden doesn't believe his bad poll numbers, and neither do many of his closest advisers."

Here's the problem: the polls consistently show Donald Trump ahead in the swing states. According to the RealClearPolitics polling average, Trump is running substantially up in Arizona (+4), Georgia (+4.8), North Carolina (+4.8) and Nevada (+5.4); he's running ahead slightly in Pennsylvania (+2.3); and he's running even in Wisconsin and Michigan. He can lose Wisconsin and Michigan and if he wins the rest, he's president of the United States.

What's more, Joe Biden's campaign has shown a remarkable unwillingness to shift course. Biden ran as a moderate in 2020, against the radical socialist Bernie Sanders in the primary and then against the purportedly unhinged Trump in the general election. That neutral image, combined with changes in the voting rules that led to an extraordinary explosion of mail-in turnout (22 million more people voted in 2020 than in 2016, an utterly unnatural increase), led to Biden's victory.

But Biden has pursued a different strategy as president. He is now widely perceived as divisive rather than uniting; his politics have swung sharply to the left; his leadership, which was always weak at best, is now perceived as completely maladroit. What's even worse, Biden's personal irascibility has risen to the fore as his presidency has stalled out; he barely leads Trump in the polling data as to whether he cares "about the needs of people like you."

That problem for Biden—the widespread belief that Democrats are disconnected from the voting public—isn't unique to Biden. Between 2016 and 2023, Morning Consult polling shows, Americans' views that Democrats care about "people like me" dropped from 43% to 31%; meanwhile, their view that Republicans care increased from 30% to 39%. A Democratic Party that *doesn't care about people* is a Democratic Party in shambles: the Big Government Party has always thrived when it has connected its heavy spending with the image of an open heart.

But Biden can't shift course. He has apparently decided to double down on the Barack Obama 2012 campaign, which relied on heavy turnout from sympathetic voting blocs rather than an appeal to moderates. That worked for Obama, but it hasn't worked for literally anyone else: Obama was a unique commodity in politics, not a model for future application. Yet Biden continues to pander to his far-left base, seeking middle ground with pro-Hamas voters in Dearborn and trans activists in Madison and BLM radicals in Philadelphia, in the vain hope that they will spur him to victory.

They won't. And so the Biden campaign is calling out the big guns: celebrities. This week, the Biden campaign, saddled with an 81-year-old, half-senile candidate, trotted out an 80-year-old, half-senile actor—Robert De Niro—to lecture the press outside Trump's campaign finance trial. It felt like the tired gasps of an asthmatic campaign.

What could Biden do to right the ship? He could start recognizing reality: that if he loses moderates, he loses the election. He could start siding with America's allies rather than catering to those who undermine them; he could begin speaking the language of individualism rather than intersectionality; he could take action to solidify our southern border rather than whining about the supposed racism of his opponents.

But he won't. So he's in real trouble, even if he refuses to acknowledge it.

Of 'Convicted Felons' and Lying Frauds

June 5, 2024

Last week, a New York City jury, prompted by the legal coordination between Manhattan DA Alvin Bragg and Judge Juan Merchan—both partisan actors—convicted Donald Trump on 34 felony counts having to do with falsification of business records. Or election fraud. Or more tax issues. Or … something. Nobody really knows, and apparently it was unnecessary for the jury to agree on the crime in order to find Trump guilty of one.

No matter.

Trump was convicted and may now face jail time. We'll find out on July 11—just a few days before the Republican National Convention. Obviously, this represents opportune timing for the Biden campaign. And yet Donald Trump remains firmly knotted with Biden in the race for the White House. There have been four polls taken since Trump's conviction. In all of them, Biden and Trump are either tied or within two points either way.

But how? The question echoes throughout the media: How can a convicted felon be running even with the incumbent president? The answer is twofold: First, Joe Biden is a truly awful president; second, Biden has no ground to stand on in labeling Trump a threat to law and order.

First, Biden's terrible record. Americans have been slammed by inflation for three years. Our social fabric has continued to decay as Biden openly seeks "equity"—meaning discriminatory legal regimens designed at rectifying group disparities—in every area of the federal government. On the foreign front, Biden has hamstrung Ukraine in its defense against Russia, and openly manipulated on behalf of Iran and Hamas in Israel's war against the terror group that performed Oct. 7. It is difficult to see an area of the world that is markedly better off since Biden took the White House.

Second, Biden's hypocrisy. In the aftermath of the Trump conviction, Trump naturally condemned the justice system that targeted him. Biden then responded by doubling down on his narrative that Trump's pushback represents a threat to Our Democracy and Our Institutions: On Friday, Biden staggered out to the podium to claim that "the American principle that no one is above the law was reaffirmed." He added that it was "dangerous" and "irresponsible for anyone to say this was rigged just because they don't like the verdict."

The problem is this: Biden as Defender of Our Democracy and Our Institutions just doesn't play. This is the same president who tried to use his Occupational Safety and Health Administration to illegally cram down vaccines on 80 million Americans; who attempted, in defiance of law, to relieve student loan debt—and then bragged about defying the Supreme Court; whose DOJ even let him off the hook for mishandling of classified material by calling him a dotard. Biden's party has spent years tut-tutting massive riots, appeasing pro-terrorist student trespassers and calling for an end to parental autonomy. There isn't an institution in the country Biden hasn't weakened. To hear Biden rail against Trump for undermining institutions, then, simply won't play. But Biden doesn't have much left in the playbook.

All of which means that Trump still—*still*—has the upper hand. Ironically, Trump being sent to jail might actually *help* him, given that most Americans will correctly see the jailing of Biden's chief political opponent as an act of vicious partisanship unworthy of the most powerful republic in world history. In 2020, Biden ran on the platform of stability and normalcy; he has exploded both. All he's left with is slogans about Orange Hitler. And that's unlikely to be enough come November if gas prices are high, groceries cost too much and the world remains aflame.

Madness in the Media

The Attack on Joe Rogan Is an Attack on Dissent

February 9, 2022

Joe Rogan must be stopped.

This is the consensus from all of the wisest and most compassionate voices in our society. According to the White House, Spotify should not merely lead off Rogan's COVID-19-centric episodes with a content warning; according to press secretary Jen Psaki, "our view is that it is a positive step, but that there is more that can be done." According to CNN's Brian Stelter, host of the ironically named "Reliable Sources": "He is now apologizing. And we're going to find out if that's enough for Spotify, the company that has an exclusive distribution deal with him." Has-been rocker Neil Young agrees; he, along with some other washed-up old hippie musicians, has taken his music off of Spotify to protest Rogan.

What was Rogan's great sin? To hear the media tell it, his great sin was COVID-19 "misinformation." Now, this is a rather vague charge, given the fact that our public health authorities have informed us over the course of the past two years that lockdowns were effective, cloth masks worked, masking of children was necessary, vaccines prevented transmission, natural immunity was inferior to vaccine immunity, and the virus could not have originated with a Chinese lab leak—all pieces of misinformation later reversed. Nonetheless, Rogan vowed to become more informed and to have on more diverse guests with regard to COVID-19 and vaccines.

When Spotify didn't deplatform Rogan over *that* charge, the rationale for his demanded deplatforming morphed: now Rogan was a racist for saying the N-word while quoting rap lyrics years ago. After a Left-wing activist group promoted a compendium video of Rogan using such language, Rogan apologized again. But apologies aren't the point. No one actually thinks Rogan is a racist. For the radical Left, you either become a tool in their arsenal or you become an object lesson. And Rogan has now become an object lesson.

He has become an object lesson for two main reasons. First, Rogan has steadfastly refused to toe the party line with regard to President Joe Biden; ire broke out against Rogan in 2020 for the crime of noting that Biden appeared "mentally compromised" in the middle of an election that the media had declared a turning point in the future of democracy. Second, Rogan has hosted guests who do not simply repeat the nostrums of the Left on a wide variety of issues. That's why the Left has demanded that Spotify remove old episodes of his show entirely: Alternative voices must not be heard, and Rogan has the unfortunate habit of talking to such voices for hours at a time and letting them say their piece.

There are several takeaways from the Rogan dust-up.

First, corporate overlords are absolutely gutless. CEO Daniel Ek believed that picking up the exclusive license to Rogan's show would increase listenership and advertising dollars; he was clearly blindsided by the blowback, to the extent that he issued a mewling letter to the company's woke interns begging their forgiveness for their hurt feelings.

Second, the media are not interested in freedom of speech as a principle. They're interested in freedom of speech for themselves and no one else. It's been fascinating to watch the evolution of our treasured Journalismers (TM) from guardians of the First Amendment to attack dogs on behalf of Big Tech censorship of their perceived enemies.

Third, apologizing to insincere radical Left alligators is always a mistake. Their goal is not a conversation. Their goal is destruction. If they find you useful, they may allow you to become Reek to their House Bolton; if they don't, you become Ned Stark to their Joffrey.

Rogan will survive all of this. Perhaps Spotify ends up paying him a bag of cash to leave, and he takes his audience and goes elsewhere, tanking Spotify's stock price on his way out the door. That would be precisely what Spotify deserves for their cowardice. But no matter what happens, the lesson will be learned by those who don't have Rogan's audience: shut up or face the whirlwind. And most will shut up.

The Slap Heard Around the World

March 30, 2022

This week, Will Smith—perhaps the most bankable star of his generation—won an Oscar for Best Actor for "King Richard." But that wasn't why he made headlines. He made headlines because during the Academy Awards ceremony, comedian Chris Rock told a joke about Smith's wife, Jada Pinkett Smith. Jada, it seems, suffers from alopecia; Rock, presumably not knowing about her condition, made a joke about her starring in "G.I. Jane 2," a nod to her closely shaven head. Initially, Will Smith laughed. Then he glanced around and saw Jada was upset.

At which point he got up, strode to the stage, and proceeded to slap Rock directly across the face.

Then he sat down again.

Rock, for his part, tried to play off the situation as a joke. But Will Smith wasn't letting it go. Instead, he began screaming at Rock: "Keep my wife's name out ya f—ing mouth!" Rock replied, "Wow, dude, it was a 'G.I. Jane' joke." To which Smith repeated, screaming, "Keep my wife's name out ya f—ing mouth!" Which, presumably, would make Rock the first man to whom Smith had ever uttered such a sentiment, given the couple's stated dedication to their open marriage.

Suffice it to say, it was perhaps the oddest incident in nationally televised history. The only rivals might have been Justin Timberlake ripping off Janet Jackson's top to reveal a pasty at the Super Bowl XXXVIII halftime show, or the live OJ Simpson car chase during the NBA Finals. But this event was even odder, given the utterly sudden nature of the assault. Rock, after all, was hired to lightly roast actors. Will Smith was there to pick up his first Oscar. And the whole thing devolved into actual violence.

It's easy to brush off the event as yet another disposably silly celebrity moment. It would be easier if Rep. Ayanna Pressley, D-Mass., hadn't immediately tweeted (and then deleted), "Thank you #WillSmith Shout out to all the husbands who defend their wives living with alopecia in the face of daily ignorance & insults." Or if Rep. Jamaal Bowman, D-N.Y., hadn't tweeted, "Teachable Moment: Don't joke about a Black Woman's hair." Or if the entire Academy Awards audience hadn't given Smith a standing ovation a few moments later. Or if there hadn't been widespread support for Smith's slap online, thanks to the now-common belief that verbal insults constitute a form of violence to which violence is an acceptable—indeed, commendable—response.

The social compact by which verbiage and violence remain strictly separated is a delicate one. For most of human history, words were treated as punishable by physical response—dueling was commonplace in societies for centuries, familial retaliation for insult was regular, and wars were even fought over verbal slights. But over time, civilized people traded away the privilege of personal use of force in favor of rules; truly offensive words could sometimes meet with social disapproval or even ostracization, but certainly not violence.

Now we seem to be reversing the trend. The entire theory of "microaggressions" suggests that if you are offended, it is because someone has "aggressed" against you—and aggression requires response. To deny someone's preferred pronouns is now an act of "erasure" amounting to violence, since the person so slighted might feel damaged in their sense of worth or authenticity. Once we reconnect the severed link between words and violence, civilization will begin to break down.

We can hope that Will Smith's slap remains an aberration; a country in which comedians are regularly assaulted for making jokes will soon be a rather humorless place. But unless Americans are willing to reestablish the hard barrier between words and violence, we will become a far more silent and far more violent nation.

Elon Musk's Twitter Takeover Reveals the Left For What It Is

April 27, 2022

This week, in one of the most shocking business moves in recent memory, Twitter reversed itself and decided to sell itself after all to Elon Musk, who paid some $44 billion for the privilege. The move was made, at least in part, for ideological reasons; Musk has been vocally critical of Twitter's management of information flow. Immediately upon the news of the buyout breaking, Musk tweeted, "Free speech is the bedrock of a functional democracy, and Twitter is the digital town square where matters vital to the future of humanity are debated. I also want to make Twitter better than ever by enhancing the product with new features, making the algorithms open source to increase trust, defeating the spam bots, and authenticating all humans."

All of these seem like worthwhile and anodyne goals. More speech, not less. More transparency, not less.

And yet the political Left went utterly insane. Charles Blow of The New York Times vowed to leave the service; in fact, #LeavingTwitter trended on the service. The American Civil Liberties Union, while noting that Musk is a card-carrying member, fretted, "there's a lot of danger having so much power in the hands of any one individual." Meanwhile, powerful individual with consolidated power Jeff Bezos worried over the possibility of Chinese influence on Twitter: "Interesting question. Did the Chinese government just gain a bit of leverage over the town square?" Sen. Elizabeth Warren called the deal "dangerous for our democracy." MSNBC's Ari Melber hilariously agonized, "You could secretly ban one party's candidate, or all of its candidates, all of its nominees, or you could just secretly turn down the reach of their stuff and turn up the reach of something else and the rest of us might not even find out about it until after the elections."

Yes, Ari, we know. That was the concern for tens of millions of us when social media decided to silence the Hunter Biden story, lock accounts of prominent Trump-associated officials who shared the story, and then finally to throw former President Donald Trump off of all services simultaneously following Jan. 6. That was one of Musk's concerns, presumably, in purchasing the service.

The Left's outsized panic over Musk's takeover is revealing for two reasons. First, it shows that the Left always understood Twitter to be a key part of its ecosystem, a Left-biased platform designed to obscure its own leanings while propagandistically pushing a particular political agenda. For years, the Left claimed that conservative concerns about Twitter bias were simple paranoia. Now, upon Musk's takeover, the Left has broken into spasms of apoplexy. That wouldn't happen if they thought Twitter wasn't their sole property.

Then there's the bigger problem: the Left despises both transparency and free speech in the political realm. The Left would prefer secret algorithms that conceal "shadow-banning" and bottlenecking; the Left prefers "equity" in speech to freedom of speech. To the Left, the potential "harm" of allowing free speech outweighs the value in open debate. Better to ban The Babylon Bee for stating that Lia Thomas is a man than to allow such content to be passed around Twitter—and better never to let anyone know the algorithms behind such bans. After all, with transparency comes accountability. And the power is the point.

This is why Musk's first moves at Twitter must be to release information about the prior practices of Twitter—a sort of truth and reconciliation commission; to make any new algorithms far more transparent; and to fire employees who object to such practices, of whom there are many. Musk may be just the man to help restore institutional trust to social media. But that will require him to bulldoze those who helped undermine that trust in the first place.

The Media's Big Lie About the 'Great Replacement Theory' and Conservatism

May 18, 2022

This week, a racist mass shooter massacred 10 people and wounded three others at a Buffalo, New York, supermarket. The shooter was a white supremacist; his hate-filled 180-page screed about why he had committed the shooting was replete with neo-Nazi sentiments. According to the shooter, he had to slaughter innocent black Americans in order to prevent the white population of the United States from being crowded out. "We are experiencing an invasion on a level never seen before in history," wrote the perverse murderer. "This is ethnic replacement. This is cultural replacement. This is racial replacement. This is WHITE GENOCIDE."

The shooter's theory, generally called the "great replacement theory," suggests that a shadowy cabal of elites, mainly Jewish, have deliberately undermined the racial purity of European countries by facilitating mass immigration and race-mixing. The shooter deliberately quoted the neo-Nazi slogan—the so-called 14 Words— "We must secure the existence of our people and a future for white children." He called himself a white supremacist, a neo-Nazi and an antisemite. Among the sources for this morally sick belief system, the shooter cited various internet sources, particularly other mass shooters who released similar manifestoes. He did not mention Fox News; he did not mention any mainstream conservative, instead stating, "conservatism is corporatism in disguise, I want no part of it."

None of this mattered to the Left-wing press, which immediately determined that the entire conservative movement was somehow guilty for the mass shooting. The New York Times headlined, "Republicans Play on Fears of 'Great Replacement' in Bid for Base

Voters." The Washington Post accused Rep. Elise Stefanik, R-N.Y., of "echo(ing) racist theory allegedly espoused by Buffalo suspect." The New Republic headlined, "The Great Replacement Theory Is Just Republican Orthodoxy Now."

What evidence did the media provide to the effect that conservatives, broadly writ, had espoused the Great Replacement Theory? They cited the belief among conservatives that the Left is generally friendly toward loose immigration in order to move the country in a progressive manner. Philip Bump of The Washington Post stated that nearly half of Republicans believed in the great replacement theory, citing a Pew poll that found that almost half of Republicans (and more than one in five Democrats) believed that "there is a group of people in this country who are trying to replace native-born Americans with immigrants who agree with their political views."

This, of course, is not the great replacement theory, which centers on racial purity rather than the idea that changing demographics have an effect on political orientation. The latter premise has been taken for granted by the Left for decades (even though it is largely faulty, as changing Hispanic voting patterns demonstrate). In fact, the Left has often argued in favor of demographic change turning the country bluer: in 2003, John Judis and Ruy Teixeira wrote a book titled "The Emerging Democratic Majority," in which they argued that Democrats were building a new electoral coalition "in which white America is supplanted by multiracial, multiethnic America"; in 2012, Greg Sargent of The Washington Post observed, "The story of this election will be all about demographics ... Rather than reverting to the older, whiter, more male version (of America's electorate) Republicans had hoped for, it continues to be defined by what Ron Brownstein has called the 'coalition of the ascendant'—minorities, young voters, and college educated whites, particularly women"; in 2013, the Center for American Progress stated, "Supporting real immigration reform that contains a pathway to citizenship for our nation's 11 million undocumented immigrants is the only way to maintain electoral strength in the future."

The goal here is obvious: conflate Republican positions with white supremacy in order to drive votes away from them. It's poisonous politics, and it happens to be a lie. But truth is of little or no priority when it comes to Left-wing politics, which are rooted always and forever in the idea that those who oppose their favored policies must be destroyed with any tool at hand.

Why the Legacy Media Is Panicked About Elon Musk's Twitter Takeover

November 11, 2022

It has now been a week since Elon Musk took over Twitter, and the wailing and gnashing of teeth is still audible across the legacy media landscape. In one sense, that's rather shocking: Why, precisely, should members of the media be so apoplectic about a billionaire taking over a social media company from other millionaires, pledging to loosen restrictions on dissemination of speech? In another sense, the outrage is perfectly predictable: The legacy media oligopoly is now under threat.

To understand the angst of the legacy media and the Democratic Party over Musk's takeover of Twitter, it's important to understand the oligopolistic history of legacy media dominance. Until the 1990s, virtually all Americans had to rely on just a few major legacy media sources: the three networks, The New York Times, WaPo and the like. A huge number of Americans relied on local newspapers, but these newspapers in turn relied on wire services like the Associated Press, AFP, Reuters or McClatchy.

This oligopoly meant both market share and control of the narrative.

The rise of the internet changed everything.

After Drudge Report broke former President Bill Clinton's Monica Lewinsky scandal, the nature of the media changed entirely. There had been hints of a brewing dissent in the works—talk radio, the rise of Fox News. But the internet shattered legacy media dominance entirely. People began diversifying their news diets en masse. The legacy media were suddenly being called out and fact-checked by outlets that people actually read.

In the early stages of the new media, people accessed their

favorite websites directly. They bookmarked these sites, and they clicked on them each morning.

Then came major social media. Social media re-centralized the mechanisms of distribution for news. Instead of bookmarking 10 websites, for example, people followed 10 accounts on Twitter, or added them to their Facebook newsfeeds. This was highly convenient—and it was good for a lot of nonmainstream news outlets, who suddenly had access to billions of eyeballs. A thousand flowers bloomed.

And, for a time, there was stasis: Because Democrats maintained political control, these social media sites were praised for their free speech principles, and clever use of these services—a la the Obama campaign in 2012—was considered good and worthy.

When former President Donald Trump was elected in 2016, however, legacy media outlets and the Democratic Party panicked. They thought they had forged an unbeatable electoral coalition; there was simply no way Hillary could have lost legitimately. Someone had to be blamed. The answer was obvious: right-wing "misinformation" and "disinformation," spread by social media, was the culprit.

The legacy media and their Democratic friends now began to blame Facebook and Twitter. Pressure was put on the social media sites to stop acting as free platforms for dissemination of a broad variety of views; instead, the social media platforms—which had monopolized news traffic—could be used to reestablish Left-wing legacy media oligopoly. Pressure even came from the Department of Homeland Security, as The Intercept reported this week: DHS engaged in "an expansive effort … to influence tech platforms."

"Misinformation" would be fought by shutting off the traffic spigots on non-legacy media; legacy media would be promoted and elevated. And because virtually all news traffic to sites now came through these social media sites, the oligopoly could once more take hold.

People were banned for saying the obvious: men were not women; mass masking was not an effective solution to COVID-19 transmission; vaccine mandates were ineffective because vaccines did not stop transmission; black Americans were not being systemically targeted by law enforcement based on race. By simply claiming victimhood, the Left leveraged social media into restricting the flow of information.

This is why Elon Musk's purchase of Twitter presents such a threat.

Musk will presumably again allow a thousand flowers to bloom. And the oligopoly can't handle that, which is why they have declared all-out war on Musk.

But it won't work. Because all he has to do is say no. We can only hope that other social media bosses follow Musk's lead and find again the mission that led them to found their companies, rather than cowering in the corner at the behest of the Democratic-legacy media complex.

Satan Is So Hot Right Now

February 8, 2023

This week, the Grammys were held in Los Angeles. They featured a star-studded cavalcade of singers who can't sing, songsters who require a team of dozens to write their songs and dancers who can't dance. They also featured a full-on satanic ritual onstage, starring used-to-be-just-a-gay-dude-then-genderqueer-now-gender-nonbinary singer Sam Smith and transgender female (translation: biological male) Kim Petras. Their song, "Unholy," won them Best Pop Group/Group Performance. Their performance, in which the tubby Smith donned a Satan outfit and top hat with horns while Petras gyrated in a cage surrounded by Satan-costumed strippers, made headlines for its transgressive imagery.

The goal, of course, is to tweak people of traditionally religious bent, draw a response and then act offended. "Why can't you just leave us alone?" cry our cultural elites as they demand our attention.

We're all supposed to be shocked, of course. That's the point.

But the fact that the performance is so *un*-shocking should be the true shock. The Grammys were sponsored by major corporations. Shadow president of the United States and world's greatest physician Dr. Jill Biden showed up to present an award. And CBS tweeted in anticipation of the Satanic routine, "We are ready to worship!"

But the truth is that Satan is so *in* right now.

After all, Satan's message has become our society's: personal "authenticity" requires the destruction of all traditional mores and the trashing of all intermediate institutions of Western civilization. To be "free" means to live without rules or boundaries. And our truest heroes are those who say, as John Milton's Satan did, "better to reign in Hell, than serve in Heav'n."

Milton meant his Satan to be a villain, rejecting the Good, True and Beautiful in favor of personal power. But we have followed the path of dissolute romantic poet Percy Bysshe Shelley, who argued, "Milton's Devil as a moral being is as far superior to his God as one who perseveres in some purpose which he has conceived to be excellent in spite of adversity and torture." Sure, Milton's Devil provided no good to anyone, including himself—but he stood up to the strictures of an outside, objective moral code. It was Shelley himself who argued that "religion and morality, as they now stand, compose a practical code of misery and servitude: the genius of human happiness must tear every leaf from the accursed book of God ere man can read the inscription on his heart."

How different are the musings of Shelley from the less-sophisticated musings of Smith and Petras? As Smith says, "It really is just about how I feel." Or Petras: "it's a take on not being able to choose religion. And not being able to live the way that people might want you to live ... I was kind of hellkeeper Kim."

God makes demands of us. God suggests that there is a higher Truth to which we are subject, rules and roles we ought to obey for purposes of societal strength, spiritual durability and personal fulfillment. Satan makes no demands of us beyond the surrender of our reason, our higher aspirations and our souls. Milton's Satan rebelled against God. Today, those of Godly bent are increasingly fighting a rebellion against the truly dominant spiritual power of a narcissistic culture that prizes self above all, celebrated by a transgressive monolithic culture.

What We Weren't Shown About Jan. 6

March 8, 2023

Jan. 6 was, according to White House Press Secretary Karine Jean-Pierre, "the worst attack on our democracy since the Civil War." Senate Majority Leader Chuck Schumer explained that the riot of Jan. 6 was a "violent insurrection." And in order to preserve democracy, Schumer stated, Fox News should take Tucker Carlson off the air.

What, pray tell, did Carlson do that merited the Senate Majority Leader calling for his silencing? After House Speaker Kevin McCarthy, R-Calif., granted him access to some 41,000 hours of as-yet-unreleased footage from Jan. 6, he aired a special in which he disclosed two particularly pertinent pieces of tape: first, tape showing Capitol Police apparently walking alongside the QAnon Shaman, Jacob Chansley, through the hallways; second, tape showing Officer Brian Sicknick gesturing animatedly to fellow officers after he had already been attacked by the crowd outside.

Carlson seemed to downplay the violence of the day based on the tape. He said, "A small percentage of them were hooligans. But the overwhelming majority weren't. They were peaceful. They were orderly and meek. These were not insurrectionists—they were sightseers."

Now, to be certain, a riot took place on Jan. 6. In that riot, dozens of officers were injured; some 1,000 people were arrested. But Carlson isn't wrong that tape appears to show some of the people in the Capitol wandering around aimlessly, not violently, or that the media's original portrayal of Sicknick's death—it was widely reported that he had been directly murdered by the crowd—was incorrect.

Argue with Carlson's framing all you want; I have significant disagreements with it. But it is clear that Jan. 6, as ugly as it was,

was a riot and not a "danger to our democracy"; that many of those in the Capitol were in fact gawking rather than rioting; and that the Jan. 6 committee went out of its way to present certain footage but avoid other footage. A decision was made by the Jan. 6 committee and the media to avoid the possibility of any nuance whatsoever regarding the riots. Instead, the only acceptable narrative determined that a riot was an insurrection, that insurrection threatened the overthrow of the United States, and that the insurrection continues to percolate throughout conservative circles. Any mitigating evidence to that overblown narrative was discarded.

Supposedly, the best way to ensure that narrative was to ensure silence. But Schumer's call to silence Carlson is precisely the reason Carlson's report went viral in the first place. The media-Democratic complex keeps exaggerating narratives, eliding any countervailing information, and then seeking to censor those who present such information; they keep burying evidentiary landmines hoping they won't be triggered. Then the landmines bow up, and they're shocked at the explosion.

We couldn't be given the footage, according to our media and political elites, lest we draw the wrong conclusions. Herein lies the problem: the best way to avoid the American people drawing the wrong conclusions is to present them with the full evidence, and then let them draw their own conclusions. And that's precisely what the elites in our media and the Democratic Party won't allow.

Meet the Company Trying to Control Your Mind

August 2, 2023

There's a group of people who control what you are allowed to see—the news you read, the videos you watch, the posts you engage with.

You haven't heard of them. You don't know their names, but they determine, through methods both direct and indirect, whether you are allowed to be exposed to particular messages. Their decisions can bankrupt companies, silence voices and fundamentally shift cultural norms. Who are these people and how do they do this?

Well, at the top level you have a network of global elites who have created a universal framework full of guidelines and ratings designed to enforce "approved" narratives and punish disapproved ones. It sounds like a conspiracy theory, except it isn't a secret and we're not guessing.

First, you have the World Economic Forum, the WEF, and their platform for shaping the future of media, entertainment and culture. Second, you have the World Federation of Advertisers, the WFA, who represent mega-corporations that control 90% of global advertising dollars. WFA members are a who's who of global business and include some of our recent wokeified favorites like Bud Light's parent company Anheuser-Busch InBev, Hershey, Procter & Gamble, Lego and Disney.

There is barely a billionaire Fortune 500 CEO, heavyweight philanthropist, government or woke nonprofit that isn't associated with the WEF or the WFA.

In 2019, the WFA established the Global Alliance for Responsible Media, or GARM. Within months, the WEF adopted GARM as part of its platform for shaping the future of media, entertainment and culture. GARM is a cross-industry alliance that brings these mega-corporations—the advertisers—together with Big Tech companies like Meta, who owns Facebook and Instagram; Google-owned YouTube; the CCP's TikTok; and even Snapchat and Pinterest.

This unholy alliance created something they call the Brand Safety Floor & Suitability Framework. Think of Brand Safety as a dog whistle for censorship. They say it themselves: The Brand Safety Floor means, "Content not appropriate for any advertising support." In other words, if you publish content that violates these guidelines, you will be blacklisted from 90% of the advertising revenue in the marketplace.

So, what have these global elites decided to put in their censorship framework? They started with things we can all universally agree on, like preventing the distribution of child pornography or the advocacy of graphic terrorist activity. But they don't draw the line at what is objectively criminal, abusive or dangerous. They continue expanding the guidelines to include far more subjective parameters.

For example, the framework lists subjective terms like "hate speech" as a problem. It says that anything surrounding transgenderism that they decide is dehumanizing or discussing what they deem to be a debated social issue in an insensitive way is off limits.

The framework is deliberately vague, allowing those in control to pick and choose how they enforce it and against whom.

So, how exactly do the approved narratives set by these global entities get enforced all the way down to the daily content you consume?

Well, here's how. We'll start with NewsGuard. NewsGuard is an organization that formulates ratings for American media. They rank news sites on a 0-to-100 scale based on nine supposedly apolitical criteria. These criteria are anything but apolitical. They often align with left-wing positions.

During the height of COVID-19, NewsGuard falsely labeled and downgraded 21 news sites, only well after the fact admitting that they either "mischaracterized the site's claims" about the lab leak theory—referring to the lab leak theory as a "conspiracy theory"—or "wrongly grouped together unproven claims" about the lab leak with the "separate, false claim" that the "COVID-19 virus was man-made" without explaining that one claim was unsubstantiated and the other was false.

"NewsGuard apologizes for these errors," they said. "We have made the appropriate correction on each of the 21 labels."

And when you compare their ratings of Left-leaning news organizations to Right-leaning news organizations, you see the same bias appear.

The Media Research Center, a free-speech nonprofit, studied NewsGuards' ratings. The study found glaring examples of bias by NewsGuard.

The Left's BuzzFeed managed a 100 out of 100 perfect score, despite its reporting on the Steele dossier and alleging collusion between former President Donald Trump and Russia.

The study found that The Global Times, a Chinese propaganda government outlet, scored a 39.5—that is 27 points higher than the U.S.-based conservative outlet The Federalist. Despite a scandal at USA Today revealing the publication of multiple fabricated sources in their stories and their own fact-checking operation misleading readers on the history of the Democratic Party and the KKK, USA Today maintained the 100 out of 100 rating by NewsGuard.

NewsGuard is also working with others to use AI technology to enforce Brand Safety standards at scale, by identifying scalable hoaxes and misinformation in order to streamline blanket removal. This means that the news that you read, news that is supposed to be fair and objective or at least diverse, must adhere to GARM, the WEF, the WFA and their subjective and biased standards in order to be deemed monetizable.

If you think this is only something big news corporations have to contend with, think again. Even the content you consume from independent content creators on social media platforms is subject to these globalist powers that be.

The WEF, GARM and the WFA are all actively working with social media companies to censor what they consider to be misinformation, which very often is just good information with which they disagree.

Finally, the WEF, WFA and GARM are all aggressively pouring

billions of dollars a year into news and content that drives their preferred narrative—narratives that are often counterfactual at best and harmful at worst.

When you look at the news, you need to feel as though you're getting all the information. And even if one source isn't giving you all the information, you can find another source, and all the sources together will give you a broad view of the world. But the World Economic Forum, World Federation of Advertisers and the Global Alliance for Responsible Media don't want you to have a full view of the news.

They want you to see what they want you to see. And they will work to prevent anyone from disseminating information they don't pre-approve. They are determining what you see, what you hear, what you watch. And that's dangerous.

The Barack Obama Cover-Up

August 9, 2023

This week, Tablet released a fascinating conversation with historian David Garrow, author of a massive unauthorized biography of former President Barack Obama in his early years titled "Rising Stars." By all rights, the book should have been a massive hit upon its release in 2017. Instead, it underperformed. The revelations contained therein never hit the mainstream. And that simple fact, in and of itself, demonstrates a simple reality of the modern political era: The entire press apparatus has been dedicated, since at least 2008, to the proposition that Obama had to be protected from all possible damage.

Garrow's book carried multiple bombshells for Obama. Obama's first autobiography—the egotist has already written several—"Dreams From My Father" told a story about how he broke up from a white girlfriend in his Chicago years over her failure to understand his desire for racial solidarity with black America. Actually, as Garrow's book relates, the couple broke up because Obama refused to disown black antisemitism. Furthermore, as the book uncovers, Obama wrote letters to a girlfriend in which he "repeatedly fantasizes about making love to men."

These are incredible allegations, to say the least. They were reported in the book. But as David Samuels of Tablet observes, the media were shockingly remiss in covering any of these stories: "'Rising Star' highlights a remarkable lack of curiosity on the part of mainstream reporters and institutions about a man who almost instantaneously was treated less like a politician and more like the idol of an inter-elite cult."

That was true in 2008, when the media steadfastly refused to take seriously reports about Obama's attendance at an openly racist and antisemitic church for two decades. And it's true in 2023, when the media still refuse to cover the fact that a huge number of President Joe Biden's closest aides are Obama's closest political allies. Obama resides in Washington, D.C.; all of the people who made policy for him now make policy for Biden. And yet nobody talks about the Obama influence in the current White House.

All of this is part of a broader pact on the part of every major apparatus in American life to mirror Obama's perceptions of the world. In Obama's own mind, he was a world-historical figure; that's why, in 2010, when he experienced a rather predictable shellacking in a midterm election, he responded by suggesting that his opposition was actually motivated by vicious racism and brutal bigotry. The media mirrored that perspective; so did entertainment; so did tech companies. The immaculate, solid wall of support for Obama's intersectional coalition is intimately connected to direct allegiance from the movers and shakers toward the Obama persona.

Just as our institutions were shaped for decades beyond JFK's death by the myth built around him, so our modern institutions will be shaped for decades to come by the myth of Barack Obama. Garrow concludes about Obama: "He has no interest in building the Democratic Party as an institution. I think that's obvious. And I don't think he had any truly deep, meaningful policy commitments other than the need to feel and to be perceived as victorious, as triumphant." But that victory—that triumph—came at the expense of the American people, who were promised a racial conciliator and a man of honor by a media invested in that lie. When the truth materialized and our institutions continued to perpetuate the lie, our institutions collapsed. We live in the era of Barack Obama still.

The YouTube Unpersoning of Russell Brand

September 20, 2023

This week, The Times of London and Channel 4 issued a scathing expose about actor and comedian-turned-podcaster Russell Brand. Brand began his career as a comedian and MTV host; in 2004, he joined "Big Brother's Big Mouth" on Channel 4, and then transitioned into acting and voice-overs. In 2013, he went political; by 2020, he had launched a successful podcast, taking heterodox positions on matters ranging from COVID-19 to the Ukraine war.

Over the course of this time, Brand also changed his personal behavior. He was a drug abuser in the early 2000s; by 2003, he was a self-declared sex addict; today, he is married with two young children.

The Times and Channel 4 report concerns behavior during the period 2006-2013. Those allegations come from five women, four of them anonymous, who accuse Brand of behavior ranging from emotional abuse to sexual assault and rape. Metropolitan Police have urged any victims to come forward. Brand denies all of the allegations.

Full disclosure: I've interviewed Russell and been interviewed by him at length. I consider him a friend. You can never truly know another person well enough to rule out vile, despicable, criminal behavior in their past; I didn't know Russell during his most debauched period, and I assume that if I had, we wouldn't have gotten along. And the allegations, as Brand himself says, are incredibly serious. Presumably we will find out all the facts as time goes on.

There is a question worth asking here, aside from the obvious question about Brand's alleged crimes: What prompted the media to begin digging into Brand? It was an open secret in Hollywood that Brand was a sexual degenerate throughout the 2000s; the media were utterly unconcerned about such matters. In fact, the same media outlets now investigating Brand were happy to make money off of him as he engaged in overtly vile behavior he himself would now be ashamed of.

So what changed? Brand did. He began taking political positions that contradicted many of the most cherished assumptions of the media class. He spoke out on a variety of issues that were considered taboo. He abandoned his past embrace of debauchery and began promoting more honorable personal behavior.

This prompted an investigation that, if the allegations are true, should have happened more than a decade ago. That investigation has now been utilized as a predicate to unperson Brand before he even responds to the allegations in full. He has not been arrested and charged, let alone convicted of a crime. Yet YouTube announced on Tuesday that it would cancel all monetization of Brand's videos on the site, preventing Brand from earning an income from any content posted on YouTube. "This decision applies to all channels that may be owned or operated by Russell Brand," the social media service explained.

Allegations can now be utilized to erase unpleasant people from social media—presumably because of what they have done in the past, but really, because of what they say now. There are reams of allegations about a bevy of YouTube creators. But those who are demonetized seem to be of one political type.

This is dangerous stuff, no matter what emerges about Brand. If he's guilty, he will pay for his crimes. But the preemptive destruction of his career makes for a truly ugly incentive structure. And it is now just one more reason for those who do have heterodox opinions to avoid speaking up.

Why The Media Despise Javier Milei

November 22, 2023

So, Javier Milei is extremely scary.

That's what the legacy media have decided: The newly elected libertarian conservative leader of Argentina is absolutely frightening. Axios calls him a "far-right libertarian who's been compared to (former President Donald) Trump." The New York Times writes, "Argentina Braces Itself for Its New 'Anarcho-Capitalist' President," and called the election Argentina's "Donald Trump moment." "Who," asks The Washington Post, "is Javier Milei, Argentina's far-right president elect?"

This, unsurprisingly, is not the way the press treated the election of former convict and Left-winger Luiz Inacio Lula de Silva in Brazil. "Brazil Elects Lula, a Leftist Former Leader, in a Rebuke of Bolsonaro," The New York Times reported last year. "Who," the Washington Post asked, "is Lula? What to know about Brazil's president."

Milei, as we've said, is one scary character.

So, what are his deeply frightening positions? He has called for vast cuts to Argentina's government—a necessity, since Argentina has defaulted on its debts three times since 2001, has a $43 billion outstanding loan to the International Monetary Fund, and now faces another default. They received a $57 billion bailout just five years ago. Thanks to out-of-control spending, Argentina has had to print pesos hand over fist, which is why, according to the Ministry of the Economy, total money supply in Argentina skyrocketed 30.7% a year from 2007 to 2022. The poverty rate in the country is 40%.

Milei's media appearances may be colorful, but that all serves a purpose: a determination to make massive change to Argentina's economic trajectory. Milei has promised to slash and burn his way through government, cutting 11 of 19 departments of the government; he campaigned with a chainsaw he pledged he would use on the "parasitic state." He wants to draw closer to the United States and Israel, and away from China. He wants to dollarize the economy.

All of this should be treated as good news. Argentina's trajectory has been a total disaster area for decades, despite the glorification of Peronism at the hands of Hollywood. And, in fact, the markets are treating Milei's election as they should: Argentine stocks and bonds have jumped on Milei's election, mainly because he is the first leader of Argentina in generations who has a plan to actually avoid economic default.

So, why the heartburn?

Because the reality is that there are many in the United States and Europe, particularly on the political Left, who somehow feel more comfortable with the socialist radicalism of Lula De Silva, Gabriel Boric and even Nicolas Maduro than with anyone who smacks of libertarianism or conservatism. That's because Argentina is a living example of what happens when corporatism and social democracy are taken to their limits: the substitution of governments for markets, the overregulation of industry in pursuit of social redistributionism, the attempts to create autarky via tariff protections and trade restrictions—the endless populist promise that if all power is given to the government to protect "the people," all will be well. That promise always results in privation and misallocation, in tyranny and poverty.

Milei's victory represents that realization.

So Leftists hate Milei.

Now the media and the political Left will attempt to shovel all of Argentina's failures on Milei's shoulders. Milei still faces a partly Peronist legislature, as well as a court system stacked in favor of Leftist foolishness: The Supreme Court magistrate Horacio Rosatti recently said that any attempt to dollarize would be unconstitutional. This means that his power may be curbed; he still faces entrenched economic problems, and he will require an infusion of foreign capital in order to right the ship in Argentina. If he comes up short, capitalism and economic liberalism will be blamed for the failures of Peronism. That's always the pattern: corporatists ruin economies, and then capitalism gets the blame.

But Milei can succeed. Investors ought to look south, to put their money where their mouth is, to ensure that Argentina realizes its potential as a massive source of prosperity, wealth and power—and that alliance with the United States grows stronger as a result.

Policy Problems

The Great Re-Sorting Is Here

January 12, 2022

This week, the incoming New York City Mayor Eric Adams—the supposed rational corrective to uber-radical outgoing Mayor Bill de Blasio—announced that he would allow legislation to proceed allowing local voting for 800,000 noncitizens. The same week, the legislature in California took up a bill that would establish single-payer health care in the state, paying for the increase in costs by essentially doubling taxes.

Americans have been fleeing the most liberal states in mass numbers. Those numbers are about to increase even more.

Between July 2020 and July 2021, approximately 352,198 residents of New York State embarked for warmer climes. Over that same period, the District of Columbia lost 2.9% of its population. California lost 367,299 people via net domestic migration. Illinois, another failing blue state, saw a net domestic out-migration of 122,460 people.

Where did all these blue state refugees go? To red states, of course. Texas picked up 170,307 Americans migrating from other areas. Florida picked up 220,890 people. Arizona picked up 93,026. Idaho had the fastest annual population increase in the nation.

The only region of the country to gain population was the South, which now holds 38.3% of the total population of the country—and which picked up 657,682 Americans migrating from different areas. The Northeast is now the least populous region in the United States, and saw a net population decrease of 365,795 residents. All net increase in population in the West was due to births and international migration, not domestic moves.

It's not just individuals—it's companies. Facebook's parent company, Meta, just signed the largest-ever lease in downtown Austin for floors 34 through 66 of the tallest tower in the city. Elon

Musk has relocated his company headquarters to Texas. My own Daily Wire relocated in 2020 from California to Nashville, Tennessee.

In other words, red state governance is a magnet; blue state governance is a disaster. Yet blue states cannot change course. They cannot simply jettison their adherence to failed ideas like single-payer health care or voting for illegal immigrants. To do so would be to acknowledge error. And so instead, they are banking on unearned moral superiority—virtue signaling—to fill the gap where good governance should be. Thus, red states are grandma-killing hellholes (where blue state legislators vacation); red states are brutal suppressors of voting rights (where Stacey Abrams wants to run for governor again); red states are filled with vicious dog-eat-dog trickle-down capitalists (who must be taxed to pay for national spending programs).

None of this is bound to convince Americans to vote Democrat. It's not designed to do so. Democrats have banked on a consistent electoral strategy since former President Barack Obama's 2012 victory—the strategy of driving out a base comprised of minority voters and college-educated women. But that strategy is collapsing—as Ruy Texiera, once the nation's leading proponent of that strategy, admitted in November, "if Hispanic voting trends continue to move steadily against the Democrats, the pro-Democratic effect of nonwhite population growth will be blunted, if not cancelled out entirely, and that very influential Democratic theory of the case falls apart."

It's falling apart in real time. But Democrats can't pull out of the tailspin. They're too invested in the lie that their programs are popular to notice how many Americans are calling up U-Haul.

Yes, It's Biden's Inflation

April 13, 2022

This week, America received news of yet another shocking inflation report: over the past 12 months, inflation has skyrocketed 8.5%, outpacing wage gains by 2.9%. That inflation has flooded every area of American life, from gas (up 48%) to airfare (24%) to furniture (16%) to milk (13%). Inflation is costing the average American family hundreds of dollars per month—and, as we know, inflation is a highly regressive tax, harming those at the bottom of the income spectrum the most.

For its part, the Biden administration blames Russian President Vladimir Putin's invasion of Ukraine. White House press secretary and incipient MSNBC employee Jen Psaki announced, "we expect March CPI headline inflation to be extraordinarily elevated due to Putin's price hike," and blamed gas prices alone for the spike. That, of course, is ludicrous. In February 2021, the month after Biden took office, the inflation rate was just 1.7%. In April 2021 it spiked to 4.2%. By May 2021, the inflation rate was 5%; it remained in that range until October 2021, when it spiked to 6.2%; it then spiked again to 6.8% in November 2021 and 7.5% in January 2022.

In other words, the problem ain't Putin.

It also isn't supply chain issues alone. The core inflation rate in Europe has remained well below that of the United States; the harmonized index of consumer prices (HICP) was 5.9% in February 2022 in the Europe area, compared with 7.9% in the United States.

So, what *is* the problem? The problem lies in loose monetary policy from the Federal Reserve for years on end, combined with wildly irresponsible economic policy from the Biden administration. Begin with the Federal Reserve. Between 2008 and 2015, the Federal Funds Effective Rate was essentially zero. It rose to 2.39% in May 2019, then dove back down to zero amidst the COVID-19 recession. This means that the Federal Reserve essentially subsidized borrowing and spending for years on end.

But the problem didn't stop there. During the COVID-19 downturn, the Federal Reserve purchased some $4 trillion in assets, injecting liquidity into the economy in the mistaken belief that the problem was lack of demand, not lack of supply. This superheated the economy; as supply chains attenuated, prices rose dramatically.

All of this was accompanied by ridiculously spendthrift policy from the Biden administration. The Trump administration, along with a bipartisan contingent in Congress, spent nearly endless amounts of money as the American economy was subjected to an artificial coma. But the Biden administration entered office with a working vaccine and COVID-19 on the wane—and then proceeded to inject trillions more in spending into the economy. In 2020, the government spent approximately $6.6 trillion in federal outlays; in 2021, the year of recovery, the government spent $7.2 trillion.

That spending was wildly unjustifiable. With vaccines available and people going back to work, the Biden administration had a responsibility to leave the economy alone. Instead, Biden insisted on reshaping the economy according to his whim. As Ezra Klein lamented to former Treasury Secretary Larry Summers, "there was a reason the Biden administration wanted to run the economy hot … it felt, finally, like we were reaching people on the margins. We were putting a lot of firepower to do that … And then for that to turn into this horrifying inflation problem, which is now eating back those wage increases … I recognize the world doesn't have to please me, but it is maddening."

Yes, reality is maddening. But not quite as maddening as the predictable results of ignoring financial reality, then lying about it in order to blame someone else.

Joe Biden's Economy Is a Disaster

June 15, 2022

This week, the stock market took a turn into bear territory on the heels of yet another brutal monthly inflation report. With the Federal Reserve considering larger rate hikes in order to tamp down record inflation, the possibility of a near-term recession now looms quite large, despite the feeble protestations of Treasury Secretary Janet Yellen. As former Clinton Treasury Secretary Larry Summers—the man who predicted President Joe Biden's inflation—stated, "I think when inflation is as high as it is right now, and unemployment is as low as it is right now, it's almost always been followed, within two years, by recession."

All of this was perfectly predictable. Firehosing money into an already-hot economy was a recipe for inflation—and yet that was precisely the policy pursued by the Federal Reserve and the Biden White House. According to The Wall Street Journal, the Biden White House and the Fed thought that the post-COVID-19 period would follow the 2007-2009 pattern: "weak demand, slow growth, long periods of high unemployment and too-low inflation." This was incontestably preposterous. The 2020 economic crash was not the result of systemic flaws in the economy like the 2007-2009 subprime mortgage crisis; it was the result instead of an artificially induced economic coma, supported by an unprecedented infusion of government cash, preceded by a historic economic boom.

This meant that when vaccines became available, when Americans headed back to work, when children went back to school, we should have been poised for an explosion in demand. To instead predict weak demand, and to build an extraordinary framework of continuing fiscal and economic stimulus on that basis, was an act of either total insanity, epic stupidity or purposeful malice. Perhaps it was a combination of all three. As the Journal observed, "many

Democrats saw their control of the White House and Congress as a rare opportunity to shift Washington's priorities away from tax cuts favored by Republicans and toward expensive new social programs." Or, as Biden himself put it this week, "I don't want to hear any more of these lies about reckless spending. We're changing people's lives!"

They sure are. It turns out that "experts" in the back room constructing a supposedly better world rarely consider the possibility of unpredicted side effects. They are so busy building glass castles in their minds that they neglect the realities of human behavior. The result is generally that those the "experts" seek most to help are actually those harmed the most.

But the Biden White House refuses to change course. Instead, they insist that the American people are too foolish to understand just how good they have it; that the answer is more government spending; that the Federal Reserve, whose loose monetary policy prompted the current price spiral, will magically draw the proper balance between rising interest rates and low unemployment.

The real answer to America's current economic woes is simple, and the same as it ever was: Leave Americans alone. Stop pumping money. Stop subsidizing boondoggle projects directed at bolstering political allies. And stop pretending that our supposed intellectual superiors have the ability to predict, control and boost an economy comprised of 330 million citizens, all of whom are better qualified to make decisions for themselves than an incompetent and incoherent president and his unjustifiably arrogant lackeys.

Why We Can't Have a Nice Independence Day

July 6, 2022

On July 3, 1776, shortly after the approval of the Declaration of Independence by the Second Continental Congress, John Adams wrote to his wife Abigail. "I am well aware of the Toil and Blood and Treasure, that it will cost Us to maintain this Declaration, and support and defend these States," Adams wrote. "Yet through all the Gloom I can see the Rays of ravishing Light and Glory. I can see that the End is more than worth all the Means. And that Posterity will tryumph in that Days Transaction, even altho We should rue it, which I trust in God We shall not."

That trust was justified in its time and ever more justified over the course of subsequent centuries. The United States has been an unprecedented, incomparable boon to humanity. It is the most powerful country in world history. It has freed millions around the globe, raised billions from poverty and shaped the destiny of entire countries and continents around the principles of the Declaration of Independence.

And now, it seems to be falling apart.

On July 4, National Public Radio abandoned its traditional reading of the Declaration of Independence in favor of a discussion of "equality." Paul Waldman of The Washington Post wrote that it was time to "declare our independence from the Founding Fathers," explaining that the "America of 1789 becomes a prison the conservative justices (of the Supreme Court) can lock us all in whenever it suits them." The Associated Press observed, in the aftermath of another mass shooting in Highland Park, Illinois, "A shooting that left at least six people dead at an Independence Day parade in a Chicago suburb rattled Monday's celebrations across the

U.S. and further rocked a country already awash in turmoil over high court rulings on abortion and guns as well as hearings on the Jan. 6 insurrection."

And, according to Gallup, this July 4, the lowest number of Americans in recorded polling history identified as extremely proud to be American. That number breaks down in highly partisan fashion: 58% of Republicans say they are extremely proud to be American, while just 26% of Democrats do. That gap is consistent across time. But for everyone—Republicans, Democrats and Independents—the number has declined.

There is a reason for that: we no longer have a common vision of what it means to be an American. From the Right, it seems that the founding principles of the nation, as articulated in the Declaration and Constitution, are under attack; therefore, pride in America has declined, particularly since 2019. From the Left, the founding principles themselves are the problem; movement away from those principles has coincided with increase in Democrat pride, which means the Trump and post-Trump era (2017 onward) correlates with an extraordinary drop in pride in America.

All of this materializes in the constant polarization of nearly every issue. For communities with a shared set of principles, individual maladies do not represent deeper philosophical cancers; for communities with heterogenous principles, every malady can be attributed to cancerous divides multiplying and manifesting. Thus, every mass shooting turns into a referendum on deeper American divides, rather than into conversations about best political policy; every Supreme Court decision turns into a debate over whether America ought to overthrow all existing institutions or to reinforce them.

Under those circumstances, America looks very much like a nation reverting to an Articles of Confederation—a loose alliance of states with little common interest outside of preserving open conflict—and less like a nation governed by a common philosophy under founding ideals. And that means that the Fourth of July will become less and less important in public life. After all, if we are supposed to celebrate what we share, and if we share nearly nothing, what precisely do we celebrate?

The Chinese Know We're in Cold War II. It's Time for Us to Understand the Same.

July 27, 2022

This week, the Chinese government announced its fierce opposition to Speaker of the House Nancy Pelosi, D-Calif., visiting Taiwan. Chinese Foreign Ministry spokesperson Zhao Lijian said that China was "fully prepared ... If the U.S. is bent on going its own way, China will take firm and strong measures to defend national sovereignty and territorial integrity." In response, the Biden administration announced its discomfort with Pelosi's visit: Biden told journalists that military officials thought the trip was "not a good idea."

Meanwhile, The Wall Street Journal reported that the Chinese government had accelerated its push to reshore the manufacture of semiconductors. According to the Journal, "China is leading the world in building new chip factories, a step toward achieving more self-sufficiency in semiconductors that could eventually make some buyers reliant on China for many of the basic chips now in short supply." That news ought to be disquieting for those who understand the flow of semiconductors, the single most important commodity on the planet, a component of nearly every major technology used today. Taiwan manufactures approximately 92% of advanced semiconductors; South Korea manufactures nearly all of the rest.

China's dependence on foreign semiconductors is one of the world's best hedges against Chinese attacks on Taiwan: should China attack Taiwan, Taiwan could destroy its semiconductors and infrastructure. But if China can ramp up its own domestic manufacture while everyone else is behind, China is in a solid position to blackmail the world economy in the same way Russia has using its energy supply.

And China isn't unaware of their growing advantage. Gen. Mark Milley, chairman of the Joint Chiefs of Staff, said the Chinese have become far more aggressive in recent years; international relations expert Shi Yinhong, who works at Beijing's Renmin University, told the Associated Press that China "will take unprecedented tough measures and the U.S. must make military preparations" if Pelosi should visit.

So, what ought the West to do?

First, the United States must stop acting as though China will change its tack any time soon. Xi Jinping has upped the ante over recent months in advance of his next party congress; he is likely to continue upping the ante as his economic and demographic model turns upside down. The long-term future for China is dismal: China's economy is a paper tiger rooted in debt, and China simply doesn't have the population growth necessary to support its massive spending. This means that China sees its window for action closing.

Second, the United States must realize it is already in a Cold War II with the Chinese government. This means ramping up our own domestic economic capacity—unleashing the economy through deregulation, energy production and tax reduction; refunding the military at the levels necessary to sustain a two-front war, and rebuilding the navy, which has shrunk to ship numbers lower than the United States had preceding World War II; diversifying supply chains for goods and services necessary to the United States, reshoring those supply chains away from China; and cutting off China's access to cutting-edge technologies.

This also means that the United States must refocus its energy and ire externally rather than internally. Americans have expended an enormous amount of time, money and energy on attacking one another, on turning inward; the result has been a cancerous politics that results in the continuing dissolution of our social capital. During the Cold War, most Americans understood that the enemy wasn't at home, it was the communist tyranny threatening the U.S. and her allies; during Cold War II, Americans must learn the same lesson again.

Buzzword Foreign Policy Makes for Failure

August 3, 2022

This week, House Speaker Nancy Pelosi went to Taiwan, determined to make a statement about American support for the democratic country under constant threat from its tyrannical Chinese neighbor. That trip prompted spasms of apoplexy from the Chinese government, which vowed serious consequences; China, in the end, engaged mainly in some military posturing.

There is no question that Pelosi is correct about the need for the West to support Taiwan, nor is there any question that China is an aggressive dictatorship. But Pelosi's trip represents the latest in a long line of American foreign policy moves that seem like bluster rather than strength. It's one thing for John F. Kennedy to fly to Berlin in the midst of a Cold War blockade of the city to show solidarity with Germans in the face of Soviet aggression, declaring that the United States would indeed defend West Berlin in case of invasion. It's another for Pelosi to fly to Taiwan in provocative defiance of Chinese caterwauling without any firm deliverable: no statement of American intention to defend Taiwan in case of invasion (President Joe Biden actually stated that America *would* do so, before his State Department then walked it back); no major increase in military aid to the island; no increase to the projective power of the United States Navy, which will purchase nine ships this year while losing 24.

Pelosi's visit, therefore, sounds a lot like the virtue signaling in which American politicians of both parties have engaged for decades. These politicians say they will protect democratic allies, then abandon them when the going gets tough; they explain that their foreign policy priorities range from free elections to gay rights, then hobnob with the world's worst dictators. They speak loudly and carry a wet noodle. Their addiction to high-flown rhetoric and vacillating commitment undercuts both their credibility and their capacity for moral suasion.

Biden represents a paradigmatic example of this sort of politician: in February 2002, for example, he stated that "history will judge us harshly if we allow the hope of a liberated Afghanistan to evaporate because we failed to stay the course"; by 2021, Biden was pulling the plug on Afghanistan, handing the country over to the tender mercies of the very same people who presided over the planning of Sept. 11. Biden spent all of 2020 describing Saudi Arabia as a pariah over its human rights violations; by 2022, he was fist-bumping Crown Prince Mohammed Bin Salman.

The answer to a foreign policy based on buzzwords is a foreign policy based on forwarding American interests, which over the long run will indeed forward America's values. Instead of suggesting that America will defend Ukraine because of Ukraine's commitment to democracy, for example—a commitment that is undermined internally by rabid corruption—our leaders should simply tell the truth: We ought to defend Ukraine from Russia because it is in our interest to counter Russian predations in Europe, which threaten the integrity of our allies in NATO and foster more aggression from our geopolitical opponents including China. At least such a clear position would prevent the misunderstandings that arise when Western nations bluster about defending democracy, then repeatedly do nothing to do so, as the West did during Russia's invasions of Georgia and Crimea.

Such a foreign policy would be nothing new; it would be perfectly in line with the famous words of John Quincy Adams, who stated that America "goes not abroad, in search of monsters to destroy. She is the well-wisher to the freedom and independence of all. She is the champion and vindicator only of her own." America ought to know her own interests. And America ought to protect her own interests. At least then our allies and our enemies will know where we stand, rather than speculating that our rhetoric is empty.

Those Who Want to Destroy the Constitution

August 24, 2022

On Friday, The New York Times published its latest op-ed calling for the end of the Constitution of the United States. The authors, Ryan Doerfler and Samuel Moyn, teach law at Harvard and Yale respectively. They argue that the Left's progress has been stymied by constitutionalism itself. "The idea of constitutionalism," they correctly write, "is that there needs to be some higher law that is more difficult to change than the rest of the legal order. Having a constitution is about setting more sacrosanct rules than the ones the legislature can pass day to day." This, of course, orients the process of law toward the past: there are certain lines that simply cannot be crossed. And, as Doerfler and Moyn point out, "constitutionalism of any sort demands extraordinary consensus for meaningful progress."

And herein lies the problem for Doerfler and Moyn: constitutions "misdirect the present into a dispute over what people agreed on once upon a time, not on what the present and future demand for and from those who live now." The solution, they say, lies in dispensing with the Constitution entirely; the proper solution to the Constitution is in "direct arguments about what fairness or justice demands." After all, they admit, "It's difficult to find a constitutional basis for abortion or labor unions in a document written by largely affluent men more than two centuries ago. It would be far better if liberal legislators could simply make a case for abortion and labor rights on their own merits without having to bother with the Constitution."

How can the Constitution be jettisoned? The authors suggest packing the Union with more states; "reorganizing our legislature in ways that are more fairly representative of where people actually live and vote"; turning the Senate into a legislative vestigial organ, without any actual power.

At least they're saying the quiet part out loud.

The truth is that the Constitution *is* "antidemocratic," in the sense that it sets up a series of limits on what a democratically elected government can do. The Constitution is a charter of limited powers, delegated by the people and the states to the federal government; neither the people nor the state governments would ever have consented to the sort of pure populism promoted by Doerfler and Moyn. The founders deplored the idea of an unfettered federal government ruled only by popular passions. That is why they put in place a system of checks and balances to forestall mob majoritarianism. They recognized a simple truth: that the best and most responsive government presides over homogeneous interests, generally locally, and that as we abstract rule away from the people, interests diverge. This means that as government abstracts away from the people, it ought to be granted less and less power.

The Left hates the Constitution for precisely that reason. To the Left, the Constitution is a mere barrier against the utopian mission to restructure human relations, and ultimately, humanity itself. In this view, large government is to be the leveling force among human beings, cramming down the views of one half of the country on the other half. Local governance is dangerous because it might lead to diversity of viewpoint and practice; federal government is the best available tool for shaping and molding. Dispense with the Constitution's limits on the powers of the federal government, and suddenly transformational change becomes possible.

The only problem is that such a viewpoint utterly disregards the history of human relations. A government that presides over 330 million human beings with a variety of different viewpoints on core moral issues is unlikely to rule either benevolently or successfully if granted the unfettered power to flatten a multiplicity of jurisdictions and ways of life. Limits are the key to both benevolence and success in governance. Dispensing with the Constitution may sound pleasing to those who seek drastic change on the greatest scale, but drastic change of that nature typically looks more like tyranny than progress.

Unserious Leadership in A Serious Time

September 7, 2022

We live in a deeply serious time with deeply unserious leaders.

Historian Niall Ferguson has written that the "extreme violence of the twentieth century" was precipitated by three preconditions: "ethnic conflict, economic volatility, and empires in decline." It is difficult not to see such preconditions repeating themselves in this century. The West is currently tearing itself apart over concerns about birthrate, immigration and multiculturalism. Economic volatility is raging: After a decades-long reshifting of manufacturing away from the West and a reorientation toward finance and service, the hollowing out of the Western energy sector in pursuit of utopian environmentalism—all punctuated by the Great Recession, the COVID-19 mini-depression and now sky-high rates of inflation—the global economy sits on a razor's edge.

And then there is the problem of empires in decline.

We tend to think of our world as empire-free, a world of nation-states. But that's not really correct. The United States, however hesitant, is a de facto empire, even if not in the colonialist mold of the British Empire; the European Union would, in any other context, be considered a continental empire; Russia has always considered itself an imperial power, and Vladimir Putin's invasion of Ukraine represents merely the latest iteration of this claim; China has an empire of its own, not merely a nation-state—as author Ai Weiwei recently wrote, "the people who live in China or come from it are a jumble of more than 50 ethnic and linguistic groups."

The Russian empire is far past decline; it is an economic backwater armed with antiquated military systems, in grave demographic trouble. But China is the area of highest risk today. The Chinese economy underwent tremendous economic growth over the course of the last two decades, but that growth now appears to be stalling out: state-run mercantilism is not self-sustaining, and as China scholar Michael Pettis recently wrote, "China's excessive reliance on surging debt in recent years has made the country's growth model unsustainable ... (it is likely) that the country will face a very long, Japan-style period of low growth." China's demographics are entirely upside-down; its population is expected to reduce by nearly 50% by 2100. And President Xi Jinping is about to declare himself dictator for life.

In all of this, China strongly resembles Nazi Germany on the precipice of territorial aggression against its neighbors. Nazi Germany saw tremendous GDP growth, rooted largely in debt, state-sponsored mercantilism and military spending; Germany's fertility rate dropped from above 4 children per woman in 1910 to well below 2 by 1935. Nazi Germany's underpinnings were fragile; Hitler saw his window closing. Military aggression was therefore not unpredictable.

So, what would China's next logical step be? Its eyes are fixed on Taiwan. Given China's historic lust for Taiwan and Taiwan's domination of the all-important production of sophisticated semiconductors, a Chinese invasion of the island would be not at all unpredictable.

Which brings us back to the deeply unserious leadership of the West.

Faced with the prospect of ethnic tensions, economic volatility and the internal instability of China, the West is opting for weakness. Economic growth is the prerequisite for military power; moral strength is the prerequisite for internal cohesion. The West has decided, over the course of years, to abandon its commitment to economic strength, instead fighting a losing war with the climate and promising endless giveaways from the unfunded welfare state; simultaneously, the West has fallen into the self-doubt of dying civilizations, pitting its citizens against each other, labeling them "semi-fascists" and "threats to democracy." We lie somewhere between the moral collapse of Rudyard Kipling's "Recessional" (1897) and Philip Larkin's "Homage to a Government" (1969). This doesn't mean that the West is on the verge of collapse; China is far more vulnerable than we are. But it does spell a future of chaos and difficulty—the kind of chaos and difficulty only strength, economic and military and moral, can successfully keep at bay.

Forgetting 9/11

September 14, 2022

On the 21st anniversary of Sept. 11, President Joe Biden repeated the same tired nostrums we have heard for the past several years on the anniversary of the worst terror attack in American history: "We will never forget, we will never give up. Our commitment to preventing another attack on the United States is without end."

That, of course, was rather ironic coming from the president who surrendered Afghanistan to the Taliban, the very people in charge of the country when al-Qaida launched its attacks on the World Trade Center and Pentagon. It was Biden who declared his own heroism as he ushered in the revitalization of al-Qaida itself in Afghanistan; as The Washington Post noted in August, "After the attacks of September 11, 2001, the U.S. goal was to deny al-Qaida a haven in Afghanistan. Now, it is back—and seemingly safe."

But none of this should be unexpected. Whatever lessons Americans learned on 9/11 have largely been forgotten one generation later.

On 9/11, we learned that the world is smaller than we think—that retreating from the world is not an option, and that if we do so, our enemies take advantage. One generation later, both parties encourage quasi-isolationist foreign policy reminiscent of the Clinton era, in which terrorism was treated as a law enforcement problem and the United States attempted to cut its presence abroad.

On 9/11, we learned that perceived weakness in any form— economic, military or ideological—invites aggression from our enemies. One generation later, we are deliberately destroying our own energy policy, focusing on expanded and fiscally irresponsible welfare statism, cutting our military capacity and pursuing radical ideological dissolution.

On 9/11, we learned that we have more in common than we do

that separates us. One generation later, the president of the United States speaks about his fellow citizens as threats to democracy and declares that those who don't deal with him are existential problems for the republic.

In the aftermath of 9/11, we learned that cultural and political change in foreign countries takes time, investment and blood. One generation later, we continue to pretend that democratic values will inevitably spread around the globe—that there is a "right side of history" that will simply manifest itself—and that exporting cultural Leftism is a necessary component of our foreign policy.

Overall, we learned on 9/11 that the world is a chaotic and terrible place in which the right may not always triumph and the wrong may do the decent terrible damage. One generation later, we seem to have forgotten that simple lesson, instead regressing to a sort of puerile innocence in which we are constantly shocked by brutal realities. This is not a recipe for safety, prosperity or success.

German Chancellor Otto von Bismarck once remarked, "There is a Providence that protects idiots, drunkards, children and the United States of America." If America repeats the idiocies of its past, it will have to rely on that Providence once more to protect us—for surely our leaders will not.

America's Suicidal Energy Policy Has Very Real Costs

October 12, 2022

Last week, Saudi Arabia announced, in conjunction with OPEC+, that it would be cutting oil production in the face of dropping prices. That decision came in spite of the Biden White House's lobbying in favor of increased production, which included a sycophantic visit by President Joe Biden to Saudi Crown Prince Mohammed bin Salman. In response to the Saudi announcement, the White House quickly announced that the United States would be reevaluating its relationship with the Kingdom.

Meanwhile, the White House announced that it would be "preparing to scale down sanctions" on Venezuela's tyrannical regime, according to The Wall Street Journal. The goal: increased oil production from the Marxist dictatorship via loosened restrictions on pumping for Chevron. The White House continues to keep channels open with the Iranian mullahs as well, soliciting concessions from the same regime that shoots women in the streets for failing to properly wear Islamic head coverings.

There is an obvious question to be asked in the face of this random and chaotic non-strategy: Why, precisely, doesn't the Biden administration just ramp up energy production by unleashing the power of America's oil industry? After all, America is still the world's leading supplier of oil and natural gas. And we have billions of dollars in investment sitting on the sidelines; refineries have been dropping offline and energy companies transitioning away from the precise forms of fuel that actually power the globe.

The answer is just as obvious: This administration is far more tied to its ideological predilections than to reality. Actually, reality actively *angers* this administration: when it fosters a foolish policy and predictably dire results follow, the administration's response is pique at that cause-and-effect relationship. This administration pursues green energy boondoggles while begging for energy from America's foes, watches those foes hold Europe hostage in the midst of a potential nuclear standoff—and then, of course, yells about how cruel our foes are for cutting off energy supplies to our allies. This is both unproductive and geopolitically imbecilic.

But at least it makes the leaders of the free world feel warm and fuzzy inside. And if America's enemies gain comparative power, at least we'll have the comfort of snootily lecturing those enemies on the certainty of their political isolation; as State Department Senior Advisor for Energy Security Amos Hochstein recently stated, "low income countries have seen that Saudi Arabia and Russia are colluding against them."

Odd, then, that low-income countries are disproportionately siding with Russia and Saudi Arabia. Perhaps that has something to do with the continued dedication of wealthy westerners to the proposition that the most effective energy policy for rising from poverty ought to be phased out—that the ladder to prosperity ought to be pulled up behind rich European nations in the name of sophistry spouted by Swedish teenagers who specialize in cross-generational derisive contempt.

The West has surrendered wise policy—or even simply non-suicidal policy—in favor of allegiance to pipe dreams. Then we wonder just why reality seems to keep collapsing in on us like an abandoned house.

The FTX Dog That Didn't Bark

November 16, 2022

In Sir Arthur Conan Doyle's famous Sherlock Holmes tale, "Silver Blaze", the detective investigates the case of a murder of a horse trainer. At first, investigators presume that the murderer of the trainer must have been a stranger to him. But Holmes cracks the case with the revelation that a watchdog remained silent the night of the murder—a "curious incident," as Holmes puts it, if the watchdog had been confronted by a stranger. No, Holmes concludes, the murderer must have been known to the watchdog.

We would do well to keep Holmes' "curious incident" in mind when discussing the complete meltdown of FTX, the cryptocurrency exchange run by Sam Bankman-Fried, a man who looks like he emerged from a laboratory dedicated to the manufacture of charlatans. Bankman-Fried was, at one point, worth some $26 billion; his exchange was the second largest in the world. But he also bragged about never reading books ("I think, if you wrote a book, you f—-ed up, and it should have been a six-paragraph blog post"); he lived in a "polycule"—a polyamorous semi-colony—along with nine of his executives; he wore gym shorts and T-shirts to important company events with Bill Clinton and Tony Blair; he placed at the head of human resources the girlfriend of the director of engineering and as chief operating officer his own intermittent girlfriend and as head of his associated hedge fund yet another intermittent girlfriend.

The red flags were endless.

And yet the scam continued.

In the coverage of FTX's meltdown, many in the media have been rather slow to ask a simple question: why didn't anybody notice that SBF was one of the most obvious scam artists of all time? Perhaps it's the insanity of the digital age, in which those fresh out of college can be assessed as billionaires without actually showing a balance sheet. But there's something else going on here: SBF was a key cog in a political machine dedicated to the proposition that a coalition of like-minded Left-wingers can seize the reins of capitalist enterprise and then work with friends in government to reconstruct the world.

That, after all, was what SBF was publicly attempting to do. He dumped $40 million into the midterm elections in support of Democrats; he donated $5.2 million to then-candidate Joe Biden during the 2020 election cycle. He had pledged the FTX foundation to hand out $1 billion in 2022. He did all of this in the name of supposed "effective altruism," a philosophy in which Left-wingers seek to use capitalism in order to enrich themselves, then dump the money into favored causes. "I wanted to get rich, not because I like money but because I wanted to give that money to charity," SBF told one interviewer.

"Effective altruism" is just another iteration of the World Economic Forum-approved "stakeholder capitalism" idea—the idea that CEOs owe their shareholders nothing, but the world at large their time, money and resources. There is a reason that FTX had partnered with WEF—a fact that WEF has now obscured by cleaning its website.

How many scam artists are using such "bluewashing" in order to cover for malfeasance—all the while colluding with government figures to redraw regulations that benefit them? That, after all, was SBF's biggest scam: He was an advocate of particular types of regulation that benefitted him and used both familial and business connections in order to protect his corporatism.

And *that's* the dog that didn't bark here: Where were the regulators with whom SBF was close? Where were the supposed advocates of "ethical capitalism," who posit social responsibility but whose friends seem to repeatedly be caught with their fingers in the cookie jar, dating all the way back to Bernie Madoff?

Maybe, just maybe, the problem isn't with capitalism per se, and its chief admonition caveat emptor, its belief that trust is to be earned rather than granted freely. Maybe the problem is with a cadre of supposed protectors of the public who aren't out to protect the public at all, but to hobnob with other "change agents" from Bahamian estates while patting themselves on the back for all the good they're doing.

The Left's Cynical 'Speech Is Violence' Ploy

November 23, 2022

This week, another evil mass shooter unleashed horror at a gay club in Colorado Springs, killing 5 and wounding another 25. The shooter—whose name I refuse to mention in order to disincentivize future shooters, who seek notoriety—was clearly mentally ill: Just last year, the shooter reportedly threatened his mother with a bomb, resulting in his arrest. Yet Colorado's red flag law, which could have deprived him of legal access to weaponry, was not invoked by either police or relatives. The Colorado Springs massacre, then, is yet another example of a perpetrator with more red flags than a bullfighting convention, and no one in authority willing to take action to do anything about him.

Yet the national conversation, as it so often does, has now been directed away from the question at hand—how to prevent mass shootings—and toward broader politics. Instead of seeking methodologies that might be effective in finding and stopping deranged individuals seeking murder without curbing rights and liberties for hundreds of millions of people, our political and media leaders have decided to blame Americans who oppose same-sex marriage, drag queen story hour and "family-friendly" drag shows. Disagreement with the radical Leftist social agenda amounts to incitement to violence, they argue.

Thus, NBC News senior reporter Brandy Zadrozny said, "there is a pipeline. It starts from some smaller accounts online like Libs Of Tiktok, it moves to the right wing blogosphere, and then it ends up on Tucker Carlson or ends up out of a right-wing politician's mouth, and it is a really dangerous cycle that does have real-world consequences." Michelle Goldberg of The New York Times wrote, "it seems hard to separate (these murders) from a nationwide campaign of anti-LGBTQ incitement ... They've been screaming that drag events ... are part of a monstrous plot to prey on children. They don't get to duck responsibility if a sick man with a gun took them seriously." Brian Broome wrote in The Washington Post that the shooting could not be "blamed on mental illness"; no, he stated, "It's right-wing rhetoric that sparks these nightmares ... The bottomless list of homophobes and transphobes on the right don't need to throw the rock and then hide their hands. Instead, they use someone else's hands entirely."

The Left's attempt to lay responsibility for violence at the feet of anyone who opposes the transgressive social agenda doesn't stop with blame—it extends to calls for full-scale censorship. "We're living in an environment that's driven by two things," averred Sarah Kate Ellis, CEO of the Gay and Lesbian Alliance Against Defamation. "Politicians who are using us to bolster their careers by creating division and hate, and number two is social media platforms that are monetizing hate, and especially against marginalized communities. They're—they're choosing profits over hate, and it's killing, literally killing our community." Social media, the logic goes, ought to shut down or demonetize any video disagreeing with the GLAAD agenda.

This is cynical politics at its worst. It's also nothing new. The Left routinely cites violent incidents as reason to crack down on free speech with which they disagree. As the inimitably imbecilic Rep. Alexandria Ocasio-Cortez, D-Instagram, tweeted, "After Trump elevated anti-immigrant & anti-Latino rhetoric, we had the deadliest anti-Latino shooting in modern history. After anti-Asian hate w/ COVID, Atlanta. Tree of Life. Emanuel AME. Buffalo. And now after an anti-LGBT+ campaign, Colorado Springs. Connect the dots, @GOP."

Yes, according to AOC, virtually every major mass shooting of the last seven years is the result of her political opponents—none of whom has called for violence. But in the world of the Left, disagreement is violence merely waiting to be unleashed. Which is why censorship, they believe, is the only way to achieve a more peaceful world.

China Is Using Big Tech—So Why Is the West Targeting Musk's Twitter?

November 30, 2022

This week, the Chinese government activated its vast censorship apparatus to prevent dissemination of news regarding thousands of citizens taking to the streets to protest the CCP's zero-COVID lockdowns. China has developed the world's most sophisticated and invasive surveillance scheme: According to The Wall Street Journal, police have been dispersing to the site of protests ahead of time thanks to their monitoring of internet traffic, cellphone data and messaging apps. China also has access to data from hundreds of millions of cameras, "some equipped with facial-recognition software... The government has enhanced these capabilities over the past two years as part of contact-tracing efforts to control the spread of the virus."

Such compulsion becomes necessary when a tyrannical government presides over an increasingly unhappy population. Chinese dictator Xi Jinping despises capitalism—in fact, he despises it so much that he has undercut the durability of his own economy in a bizarre quest to pursue a form of authoritarian mercantilism. The result has been slower economic growth, shoddy product innovation and extraordinary levels of debt, all piled atop an aging demographic time bomb. He has sought to make up for this through higher levels of compulsion domestically, combined with stealing technology from the West and utilizing military power to simply take over areas like Hong Kong. Chinese tech companies have been brought to heel: as The New York Times reported in July 2021, Chinese "companies and entrepreneurs are effectively telling the government that they know who the master is."

But Xi hasn't stopped there.

Xi has taken advantage of the weak underbelly of capitalism—the reality that profit-seeking enterprises will allow themselves to be co-opted by malevolent actors in order to maintain their profitability, that corporations are not predominantly concerned with American national security but with economic efficiency. This is why Apple is now reportedly doing the bidding of the Chinese government.

Apple, which bases its manufacture of the iPhone, among other devices, in China—to the point where 25% of the value of the iPhone apparently comes from Chinese companies—is completely subject to Chinese whim, and they know it. That's undoubtedly why Apple cut off its Airdrop feature in its latest Chinese update, just before the anti-lockdown protests broke out: Airdrop allows users to transfer data using wireless connections rather than the internet, which avoids governmental scrutiny.

Apple isn't a rarity. Multiple major companies have had to make the choice between access to China's markets and labor resources and standing against Chinese autocracy. Some companies have withstood the test—but not enough of them.

Meanwhile, the West is focused, laserlike, on Elon Musk's Twitter as the supposed threat to democracy. This week, the EU announced that Twitter could be in violation of the Digital Services Act, which forces social media platforms to police "hate speech." The White House has also announced that it has its eye on Musk's Twitter, which it says has now become a font of "misinformation." Musk has dedicated Twitter to opening up standards of speech, allowing those with non-lawbreaking activity to tweet.

This has raised the hackles of our thought leaders—not Apple actively doing the work of suppressing sharing of information in authoritarian China.

All of this bodes ill for the future of the digital age in the West. If the West is perfectly sanguine about tyrannical regimes weaponizing capitalism and technology while fretting over capitalists who own technology companies *broadening* the use of their platforms, the West will be contributing to its own defeat. And China will celebrate.

The Left's Big Pitch: Embrace a Worse Life in the Name of Equality

December 21, 2022

This week, The New York Times released a long expose of the shortcomings of the United Kingdom's National Health Service. Long cherished as a crown jewel of Left-wing governmental policy, the NHS has been plagued by massive resource shortcomings, requiring rationing of critical infrastructure and care. Now, citizens are waiting up to 12 hours for ambulances. "It's a near-crisis situation that experts say reveals a breakdown of the compact between Britons and their revered National Health Service," the Times reported, "that the government will provide responsible, efficient health care services, mostly free, across all income levels."

There can be only one excuse for such signal failure to serve the prosperity of your citizenry: the chimera of equality. This, in fact, is the clarion call of the Left: that human beings sacrifice well-being and prosperity on behalf of the cult of equal distribution of resources. Klaus Schwab, head of the World Economic Forum, says as much in his book, "The Great Narrative": we should dispense with economic measures like gross domestic product (GDP) in favor of "what matters most: climate action, sustainability, inclusivity, global cooperation, health and well-being." In fact, says Schwab, "We might even find we can live with such a scenario quite happily!" The end goal will be ending "inequality and the unfairness that underpins it" by enshrining "universal provision of social assistance," which will require that governments "rewrite some of the rules of the game and permanently increase their roles."

Closer to home, New York Times columnist Jamelle Bouie says the same when he argues in favor of government nationalization of all wealth and then redistribution of that wealth on a per capita basis

... every generation. This would amount to a complete rupture of property rights—and this in turn would mean the end of innovation, since societies that dispense with property rights and profit margins regress into stagnation and then economic collapse. But at least we will have achieved Bouie's goal: equality!

Indeed, members of the political Left are constantly asking citizens to simply reframe their perspectives on prosperity entirely. Jerusalem Demsas, writing in The Atlantic, calls on Americans to rethink whether homeownership is worth pursuing, explaining, "pushing more and more people into homeownership actually undermines our ability to improve housing outcomes for all." Indeed, rather than all aspiring to buy houses and some succeeding, Demsas calls for "public investment in rental-housing quality" as well as government "rent-stabilization policies." None of this will make it easier for anyone to own a home, but it will make everyone more equal in their government-sponsored tenancy.

President Joe Biden's entire economic agenda is built around the notion of economic mediocrity rooted in a self-proclaimed higher justice. Paul Waldman of The Washington Post posited this week that Biden had launched an "economic policy revolution" rooted in fighting "inequality." This would require "more active government intervention in the economy."

And we will all learn to love such intervention, because it will be done in the name of a higher value: equality. Not equality of rights, but equality of outcome; not equality of value, but equality of resources. The problem with this philosophy is that it removes the incentive for all that creates prosperity: work, creativity, thrift, responsibility. And removing that incentive means more misery for everyone.

Our Blundering, Intrusive Government

January 11, 2023

Our government seeks more and more control.

Our government is not competent.

These two statements are both true, and together amount to a nightmare for institutional credibility. A government that seeks more control must at the very least demonstrate credibility in implementing its goals; a government that is incompetent can only regain legitimacy by limiting its authority. And yet we have a government that presents the worst of both worlds: incapacity to perform its most basic functions, combined with an ever-expanding encroachment into daily life.

Thus, this week, the Federal Aviation Administration was forced to ground virtually all flights in the United States after an outage in the so-called Notice to Air Missions systems, designed to warn pilots of weather problems, runway issues or other obstacles. The NOTAM system relies on a reportedly outmoded computer system that has not been updated for years. Transportation Secretary Pete Buttigieg, who is most famous for taking a two-month paternity leave and then bragging about it repeatedly on national television, helpfully commented, "There was a systems issue overnight that led to a ground stop because of the way safety information was moving through the system." He then reported this problem to President Joe Biden, who helpfully commented that Buttigieg ought to "restore the system quickly and safely, and to determine causes."

Job well done, gentlemen.

The air traffic control nightmare is but the latest example of a government well over its skis. Whether we are talking about the nation's scattershot but brutal COVID-19 lockdown and mandate policies, its utter incapacity to handle a historically unprecedented flood of illegal immigration across our southern border, railroad strikes barely averted by congressional force or the inability to recruit members of our military, our government seems to be failing repeatedly at issues that implicate core competency.

And yet at the same time our government proves itself shockingly unable to perform its most basic functions, it continues to expand its ambitions. Thus, this week, we found out that the Consumer Product Safety Commission may consider banning gas stoves in the home, supposedly thanks to the risk of childhood asthma caused. There are approximately 40 million households in the United States currently using gas stoves.

When governments promise much but deliver little—and when they seek to control much, but only succeed in controlling the most minute and irritating aspects of daily life—they lose their legitimacy. And that is precisely what has been occurring over the course of the last century in the United States. The growth of the regulatory state means that government now reaches into the nooks and crannies of the lives of its citizens—and yet government cannot actually do the most basic things required of it. The response of citizens, unsurprisingly, is distrust in government itself.

But that distrust does not manifest, unfortunately, in widespread calls by citizens to restrict the size, scope and intrusion of government. Instead, it manifests as a cry to "elect the right people." This is a category error. The problem with our government is not one of staffing, but one of incentives—and all the incentives are on the side of inefficiency, blundering and encroachment. That is not likely to stop until the American people recognize that they can have competent government or intensely involved government, but not both. In a representative republic, the problems of government are, in the end, the problems of the people who vote for them.

Joe Biden Turns the American Government Into Wokeness, Inc.

February 22, 2023

Last week, as Presidents Day weekend loomed, the Biden administration dropped a little-noticed executive order. That executive order happened to be one of the broadest, most transformative executive orders in modern American history; it turned the federal government into one giant machine designed for the propagation of woke principles. The so-called "Executive Order On Further Advancing Racial Equity And Support For Underserved Communities Through The Federal Government"—presumably titled in jargonistic gobbledygook in order to avoid scrutiny—set out the key guiding principle for the Biden administration. This principle, "equity," will now be used to redirect the entirety of the federal government's awesome powers.

What, pray tell, is "equity"? It certainly isn't equality—the presumption that Americans ought to be treated equally under the law as individuals. Instead, equity presumes that any group disparities must be the result of perverse government policy, and that the only corrective is government interventionism. The new executive order suggests that "by advancing equity, the Federal Government can support and empower all Americans, including the many communities in America that have been underserved, discriminated against, and adversely affected by persistent poverty and inequality." Poverty, you see, is purely the outgrowth of discrimination and lack of service. Individuals must never be implicated in their own failures, nor can cultural differences justify group underperformance. As Ibram X. Kendi more bluntly puts it, "As an anti-racist, when I see racial disparities, I see racism."

The solution, therefore, is that government must correct all policy that allows for the annoyingly eternal human conditions of poverty and inequality. Biden's executive order dictates that equity be "embedded ... into the fabric of Federal policymaking and service delivery." This will not be a "one-time project"; it must instead be a "multi-general commitment, and it must remain the responsibility of agencies across the Federal Government." To that end, virtually every agency of government must establish an "Agency Equity Team ... to coordinate the implementation of equity initiatives." Every aspect of government down to the design, development and acquisition of artificial intelligence must advance equity.

Nothing gives the president of the United States the unilateral authority to reshape the entire executive branch into an agent of "equity." That is a legislative function, and the legislature has given no such grant of power. But Biden is doing it anyway. And that means stacking—presumably for generations to come—a Deep State of "equity"-driven Left-wing bureaucrats throughout the federal government, systematizing the equity agenda throughout the unelected and unanswerable areas of the executive branch.

This is dangerous, and it must be stopped. It is violative of constitutional principles, both in terms of separation of powers and under the equal protection clause—which is designed to prevent precisely the sort of group-driven resource allocation Biden favors. Stopping this executive order must become the first priority of the Republican House, and of future Republican presidential candidates.

Biden is deliberately planting a poisonous seed in the fertile soil of the world's most powerful executive branch. That seed will bear hideous fruit as the years roll by. The only answer is to uproot the seed before it begins to sprout.

How To Crash the Economy, Big Government Style

March 15, 2023

We are in a looming financial crisis, even if we don't want to see it.

Silicon Valley Bank (SVB) was, according to Moody's, worthy of an investment-grade rating as of March 8, 2023. S&P Global Ratings similarly held a high opinion of SVB. Two days later, SVB was shut down; immediately, Moody's dropped SVB into junk territory. So did S&P Global Ratings. Within days, Signature Bank—with Barney Frank, co-sponsor of the famed and much-ballyhooed Dodd-Frank Act, on the board—went belly up.

The Biden administration, touting its own heroism, immediately stepped in to fill the gap. Concerned that unsecured depositors would lose billions in cash, Team Biden announced that all unsecured depositors would get their money back; the Federal Reserve launched a Bank Term Funding Program, to create additional reserves for the banks. Then President Joe Biden himself claimed that he had stabilized the banking system.

He hasn't.

To understand just why throwing money at the problem with the banks won't solve the underlying issue, we need to understand just why SVB failed in the first place. It failed thanks to three specific factors: from 2020 to 2022, the federal government injected more liquidity into the American economy than at any time in history, bar none; SVB, trusting that the liquidity would keep on coming, socked away a large amount of that liquidity into bonds, which bore a low interest rate; the federal government, having now created an inflationary wildfire, had to count on the Federal Reserve to cut inflation by raising interest rates. Those increased interest rates made

SVB's bond holdings lower; when depositors, hampered by the lack of easy money, started to withdraw their cash, SVB had to liquidate the bonds at a loss, essentially bankrupting them.

So, what happened? Simply put, the federal government created a carousel of easy cash; investors thought the carousel would never stop; it stopped. Now, the federal government blames capitalism—and in the process, claims that by injecting *more liquidity into the system,* it will prevent capitalism from melting down the banks. But instead, the federal government has created two new problems: first, the Federal Reserve has now given itself the unenviable task of simultaneously quashing inflation (which requires raising interest rates) and shoring up the banks (which requires lowering them and/or injecting more liquidity); second, the federal government has created a new and massive moral hazard, whereby bank managers know that if they promise outsized returns to their depositors, they can gain their business—and worst case scenario, the government will bail out the depositors anyway.

Now the experts tell us that the Biden team will achieve a soft landing—that they'll somehow square the circle, lowering inflation while preventing bank assets from depreciating, incentivizing financial responsibility while simultaneously backstopping bad decision-making, promoting fiscal responsibility while proposing $7 trillion budgets. No one has this kind of power, least of all the team that's brought America four-decade-high inflation, the highest interest rates since before the 2007-2008 financial crash and an ever-soaring national debt.

No, the crisis will arrive. If it feels like the federal government can fly, that's just because it always feels that way when you jump out of a tenth-story window and you're nine stories down. Joe Biden and the economy are not immune to the forces of financial gravity.

Our Fake Spending Debates

May 31, 2023

This week, Speaker of the House Kevin McCarthy, R-Calif., and President Joe Biden cut a deal to raise the debt limit. The breakthrough came after three months of Biden pledging not to even negotiate over the debt limit. Instead, Biden was forced to concede to a 1% cap on increases for non-military spending, a cutback on IRS funding, a clawback of some unspent COVID-19 allocations, and addition of work requirements for some federal aid. The compromise deal was indeed far less than House Republicans had demanded, as Rep. Nancy Mace, R-S.C., tweeted, "After factoring in a small cut to discretionary spending over the next 2 yrs, we are still talking about ~$6T more or less in spending bc of large increases in spending elsewhere. … Govt grew massively over the past 3 years. This growth was supposed to be emergency funding only during COVID. During this time, govt grew 40% or by $2 trillion from 2019 to 2023. We went from spending just over $4T to spending just over $6T."

Every word of that critique is true. Compared to conservative ideals, the compromise bill is indeed a flaming bag of fiscal manure. But conservative ideals weren't on the table. Biden is the president. Sen. Chuck Schumer, D-N.Y.—thanks in large part to the tender 2020 ministrations of President Donald Trump in the Georgia Senate runoffs and his further interference in the 2022 Senate races in Georgia, Arizona, New Hampshire and Pennsylvania—is still the Senate majority leader. This means that Republicans were never going to get a big win on budgetary matters.

For that matter, Republicans couldn't even get a big win on budgetary matters from 2016 to 2018, when they controlled both houses of Congress and Trump was actually president. In fact, Trump campaigned in 2016 against changes to entitlement programs, which represent the biggest driver of our national spending addiction—some 62% of federal spending annually. Combine that spending with 10% of our spending on net interest and another 13% or so on defense spending, and the discretionary outlays at issue represent under $1 trillion. That's a lot of money, to be sure, but making serious cuts to that number would still put our budget in the $5 trillion range.

The reality is that our budgetary debates are generally about shifting deck chairs on the fiscal Titanic. By 2053, we will be dedicating in excess of 21% of our national budget to debt service alone. Mandatory spending will constitute 58% of our spending. We aren't going to cut our way out of this problem by targeting discretionary spending in the main.

But nobody will touch the real drivers of our budgetary bloat and economic stagnation—Social Security, Medicare and Medicaid. To do so would risk the wrath of entrenched interests in the United States. So instead, we'll simply increase the size and scope of federal spending, placing an unsustainable burden on our economy and then eventually mandating vastly increased taxes or serious austerity measures. There is no third path forward.

Our politicians know this. But they're in the business of kicking cans down the road while posturing over the placement of the deck chairs. The iceberg looms, but their reelection efforts rely almost completely on ignoring its presence as we bear down, full speed, on our fiscal doom.

The Law of Unintended Consequences Can't Be Repealed

August 30, 2023

This week, the Biden administration announced that Medicare would name some 10 prescription drugs it would subject to direct price negotiations. The drugs include Jardiance (diabetes), Entresto (heart failure), Imbruvica (blood cancer) and Stelara (psoriasis). If the companies that created the drugs refuse to kowtow to Medicare, they will be forced to withdraw from Medicare and Medicaid coverage or face a 95% excise tax.

The White House celebrated the decision as a win for taxpayers: after all, they pointed out, the 10 selected drugs were responsible for one-fifth of all Medicare Part D prescription costs between June 1, 2022, and May 31, 2023. "There is no reason," Biden said in a statement, "why Americans should be forced to pay more than any developed nation for life-saving prescriptions just to pad Big Pharma's pockets."

Of course, that's not what's really happening.

First off, drug development is unbelievably expensive. In 2019 alone, the pharmaceutical industry spent $83 billion on research and development. According to a 2020 study, which covered some 632 new therapeutic drugs and biologic agents approved by the FDA, the "estimated median capitalized research and development cost per product was $985 million, counting expenditures on failed trials." The average cost was $1.3 billion (some drugs are much more expensive to develop than others). According to the National Institutes of Health, the success rate of drug development is just 10 to 15 percent.

Americans bear the brunt of this cost—largely because other countries free ride. But Americans also capture the industry upside of drug development in the United States. This is why, according to one 2010 study, the United States accounted for "42 percent of prescription drug spending and 40% of the total GDP among innovator countries and was responsible for the development of 43.7 percent of the (new molecular entities)." According to the Bureau of Labor Statistics, the pharmaceutical and medicine manufacturing industry is responsible for some 332,000 jobs.

So, what would the new regulations do? If they are implemented, according to National Review's Jeff Zymeri, drug development will drop off: "The CBO has predicted that the scheme provided for under the IRA would lead to a manufacturer-revenue loss of 15 percent. Such a cut in CBO's predicted 45 new drugs per year would suggest around 6.8 fewer drugs per year, totaling around 121 lost over the 18-year horizon, as one report estimated." The drugs most likely to disappear would be drugs that target rare conditions and thus have less of a market.

As an investor in biotech stock, I can say with confidence that investment will shift out of the sector and into other, freer sectors should the Biden administration move to quash profit margins in the sector. Why would investors sink money into a drug, only to find out that the more successful it is, the less profit there will be in it?

There is another solution: Force other countries to pay their fair share. This would ensure that Americans pay similar prices to those around the world, while also creating incentive for innovation. But that would require politicians to abandon their happy talk and deal in the real world. And *that's* not something politicians are likely to do.

Congress' Perverse Incentive Structure

October 4, 2023

This week, a small coterie of House Republicans moved, along with all House Democrats, to oust Speaker of the House Kevin McCarthy. Led by Rep. Matt Gaetz, R-Fla., they claimed that McCarthy had to go because of his insufficient zeal in cutting spending, most prominently by failing to advance more individual spending bills.

McCarthy, for his part, had advanced four individual spending bills, which were then rejected by the Senate. In order to avoid a government shutdown, McCarthy attempted to pass a continuing resolution that would have cut discretionary spending by 8% and included border security provisions; Gaetz and his colleagues voted it down. McCarthy then passed, with a majority of Republican support plus some Democratic support, a "clean" continuing resolution to fund the government for 45 days, not including any further funding for Ukraine.

This, for Gaetz, was supposedly the last straw. He took to the floor of the House to accuse not merely McCarthy but the entire Republican caucus of cowardice in confronting President Joe Biden's spending agenda. "My colleague says we've passed the strongest bills in history, well guess what, look at the border right now … I take no lecture on asking patriotic Americans to weigh in and contribute to this fight from those who would grovel and bend knee for the lobbyists and special interests who own our leadership … who have hollowed out this town and have borrowed against the future of our future generations."

All of this would be more convincing except for two simple facts: First, Democrats control the Senate and presidency, making it impossible for Republicans to pass bills closing the border and radically cutting spending; and second, Gaetz is perhaps Congress' most ardent supporter of former President Donald Trump, who added some $7 trillion to the national debt and pledges never to touch the greatest drivers of America's debt: Medicare, Medicaid and Social Security.

So, what was this truly all about? Radically misaligned interests. The Republican Party has zero actual institutional power at this point. It can be captured from the outside with ease; it can be twisted by a few rogue actors who seek attention rather than policymaking power. McCarthy signed his own political death warrant the day he acquiesced to insurgent Republicans' demand that they be able to challenge his speakership with a single vote. Once, congressional Republicans ensured solidarity through the power of the speakership; now the speaker worries about avoiding his own demise at the hands of fractious politicians seeking TV spots on CNN and MSNBC.

This won't change with McCarthy's ouster. Should Rep. Steve Scalise or Rep. Jim Jordan take over, they will presumably still serve at the behest of a few free radicals who can ensure chaos at the drop of a hat. The only way to restore any semblance of order to the House would be to restore consequences for violating party solidarity. And that won't happen so long as conservative media declare anyone a hero who declares himself a lone man standing against the "powers that be"—and so long as both politicians and conservative media parrot the lie that if only Republicans were simply more determined, conservative policy priorities would magically become law over the objections of a Democratic Senate and Democratic White House.

Weakness Breeds Aggression

January 31, 2024

This week, three American soldiers died at the hands of an Iranian proxy group that used a drone to strike an American base in Jordan. The Biden administration immediately leapt into action by issuing a strongly worded statement, while simultaneously proclaiming that they wanted to avoid escalation. Which, of course, is precisely the wrong thing to do when faced with aggression from a smaller, hostile adversary.

The right thing to do? Punch them in the mouth hard enough to deter further aggression.

That is something President Donald Trump knew innately. On Dec. 31, 2019, Iranian-backed proxy groups stormed the U.S. embassy compound in Iraq, killing a U.S. contractor. "Iran is orchestrating an attack on the U.S. Embassy in Iraq," Trump tweeted. "They will be held fully responsible." On Jan. 2, 2020, the Defense Secretary said there were "indications" that Iran was planning "additional attacks" on American targets.

On Jan. 3, 2020, the U.S. military killed Iran's top terrorist commander, Qassem Soleimani.

This led to teeth-gnashing from the American left, which declared such an activity a major escalation. Iran blustered that the assassination was "tantamount to opening a war against Iran." Trump then threatened, "Let this serve as a WARNING that if Iran strikes any Americans, or American assets, we have targeted 52 Iranian sites (representing the 52 American hostages taken by Iran many years ago), some at a very high level & important to Iran & the Iranian culture, and those targets, and Iran itself, WILL BE HIT VERY FAST AND VERY HARD."

Iran fired some missiles at some empty sites.

That was the end of that particular exchange.

It turns out that if there is one party in the Middle East that wants a U.S.-Iran war less than the United States, it is Iran.

Which is how deterrence works.

That's what makes it so absurd that the Biden White House's first Middle Eastern goal upon taking office was to destroy deterrence against Iran. The White House first declared itself in opposition to the Saudi regime, chiding Mohammed Bin Salman over human rights violations; the White House removed the Iranian-backed Houthis from the terror list; the White House tried to reopen Iranian nuclear talks.

Despite the White House's idiocy, Sunni-Israeli peace seemed to be in the offing. In fact, as a *result* of the White House's idiocy, Saudi Arabia had drawn closer to Israel than ever before as a defensive measure against a resurgent Iran.

So Iran acted. Iran acted knowing that the Biden administration is cowardly in its approach to foreign affairs—that they're willing to slow-walk aid to American allies under pressure but unwilling to countenance the credible threats of military force by which deterrence is established. And now the Biden administration continues to vacillate. After spending the months since Oct. 7 repeating ad nauseam an admonition to Iran not to escalate its violence—"Don't!" every Biden official, including Biden himself, has repeated—Iran has indeed escalated its violence. It turns out that saying "Don't" to aggressive foreign powers isn't nearly as effective as saying "Don't, or you may not be breathing tomorrow."

Napoleon Bonaparte once supposedly stated that his military policy was an "iron hand in a velvet glove." When the iron hand disappears, replaced with fluff, there isn't much for Iran to fear. And in an election year in which the president deeply fears a further conflict with Iran, Iran isn't the party being deterred. America is, at the cost of American lives.

Involvement in Ukraine

Putin Wakes up the Western Ostrich

March 2, 2022

After the end of the Cold War, foreign policy experts across the spectrum assured us that things had changed. Wars of pure border conquest were over. Wars over oil would soon be a thing of the past. Instead, the increasingly intertwined world would move toward peace. Thomas Friedman suggested in his massive 1999 bestseller "The Lexus and the Olive Tree" that no two countries with McDonald's would go to war with each other; Francis Fukuyama stated in "The End of History and the Last Man" that we had reached the "end-point of mankind's ideological evolution and the universalization of Western liberal democracy as the final form of human government."

The West set about proving these dubious theses by embracing what could be termed an ostrich foreign policy: a willingness to place security considerations last, and to pursue utopian goals with alacrity. Germany spent decades making itself more dependent on Russian natural gas and oil in order to pursue the dream of green energy, meanwhile slashing its defense budget as a percentage of GDP. France acted similarly. So did the United Kingdom.

The West banked instead on more economic interdependence via the International Monetary Fund and World Trade Organization, more diplomacy at Davos and the United Nations.

Most of all, the West banked on its own unwillingness to recognize reality. When, in 2012, Mitt Romney made the crucial error of reminding Americans that Russia was a geopolitical foe, President Barack Obama openly mocked him. So did Obama's complaint media. The 1980s had called, and they wanted their foreign policy back.

When aggressive global competitors made clear that they did not buy into the West's vision of a grand and glorious materialist future combined with welfare statism—that they believed their own national histories had yet to be fully written, and that their centuries-old territorial ambitions were still quite alive—the West simply looked the other way. When Russia invaded Georgia in 2008, the West did nothing. When Russia invaded Crimea in 2014, the West did nothing. When China abrogated its treaty with the U.K. and took over Hong Kong in 2020, the West did nothing. And, of course, President Joe Biden precipitously removed American support for the Afghan regime, toppling it in favor of the Taliban.

The West decided that it would make a war-free future a reality by simply ending war.

Now, as the West is finding out, ending war is a game that requires two players. Russian President Vladimir Putin saw Western weakness as the impetus for his final grand strategic move: the destruction and occupation of Ukraine. And the West has been shocked back into reality: yes, opponents of American hegemony are territorially ambitious; yes, they want more than mere integration into world markets; yes, they are willing to murder and invade in order to achieve their goals. Times and technologies may change, but human nature remains the same.

As George Orwell wrote in 1940 about the rise of the Nazis, "Nearly all western thought since the last war, certainly all 'progressive' thought, has assumed tacitly that human beings desire nothing beyond ease, security and avoidance of pain … Hitler, because in his own joyless mind he feels it with exceptional strength, knows that human beings don't only want comfort, safety, short working-hours, hygiene, birth-control and, in general, common sense; they also, at least intermittently, want struggle and self-sacrifice, not to mention drums, flags and loyalty-parades."

The West rose to meet Hitler's challenge. It appears that the West is rising again to meet the challenge of Russian aggression. We can only hope that the West's newfound commitment to a very old idea—the idea that only a sense of Western purpose combined with some very hardheaded thinking about hard power can preserve freedom—lasts longer than Putin's invasion. If it doesn't, the reshaping of the world order will continue, to the lasting detriment of a West that is only now removing its head from the sand.

Environmentalist NIMBYism Means Foreign Policy Disaster

March 9, 2022

This week, as the Russian invasion of Ukraine dragged on, gas prices in America soared to their highest levels since 2008, increasing over 57 cents in just one month. In parts of the United States, gas at the pump costs in excess of $7 per gallon.

The answer to this challenge is obvious: The United States ought to open the drilling floodgates. In 2019, net imports of crude oil and finished products were exceeded by American exports of such products for the first time on record. That was due to the massive increase in American production thanks to fracking over the course of the prior decade. This did not mean that the United States had stopped importing crude oil. But as of 2019, we were importing some 3.8 million barrels of crude oil per day, radically down from over 10 million in 2005. More production, generally speaking, means less dependence.

And that matters, as we're now seeing. Europe, which is far more dependent on foreign oil than the United States, has seen its energy prices skyrocket since the Russian invasion. That's why Germany's Chancellor Olaf Scholz announced, "Europe has deliberately exempted energy supplies from Russia from sanctions. Supplying Europe with energy for heat generation, mobility, electricity supply and industry cannot be secured in any other way at the moment." U.K. Prime Minister Boris Johnson agreed: "I think there are different dependencies in different countries, and we have to be mindful of that."

So now would be an excellent time for the United States to grab muscular leadership of the world energy markets. Instead, the Biden administration—which opted upon taking office to undercut the oil and gas industry and radically subsidize inefficient "green energy" production—has decided to seek energy aid from some of the world's worst dictatorships. This week, the Biden administration sent emissaries to the Venezuelan dictator Nicolas Maduro in an attempt to increase oil imports from the socialist hellhole. White House press secretary Jen Psaki said, "The purpose of the trip that was taken by administration officials was to discuss a range of issues, including certainly energy security."

Meanwhile, Juan Guaido, leader of the Venezuelan opposition, was left out in the cold. "It is foolish to think that Maduro will quit Russia," he quite logically explained. "This is a mistake. To buy oil from Maduro is the same as buying oil from Putin."

But this is the point: For the international Left, dependency on oil-driven authoritarian states is *preferable* to energy independence. It allows Left-wing leaders the privilege of appeasing their environmentalist base while at the same time keeping energy prices low. Carbon-based emissions are too hideous to be considered so long as they're being produced on American or European soil—but we're perfectly willing to subsidize Russian President Vladimir Putin, Maduro and the Iranian ayatollahs to exploit the environment and enrich themselves while promoting tyranny at home and abroad, so long as Greta Thunberg isn't disappointed in us.

And so we continue to promote the abject idiocy of Secretary of Transportation Pete Buttigieg, who recommended to those suffering from high gas prices that they just shell out for an electric vehicle. We continue to nod along to the stupidity of Psaki, who agreed that the solution to $7-a-gallon gas was "getting the whole country off of fossil fuels." Then we import our energy from the world's worst despots.

Opposition to oil and gas development has always been the privilege of rich countries; we simply outsourced the pollution and environmental degradation elsewhere. But as it turns out, in the end, we all pay the price for our willingness to pay off autocrats just so we can temporarily pretend that we did our bit for Greenpeace.

Push Where There's Mush

March 16, 2022

There is no substitute for American strength. When America's enemies find weakness, they exert pressure. And today, America's enemies are finding weakness at nearly every turn.

Vladimir Lenin supposedly stated that his preferred foreign policy strategy was to "probe with bayonets: if you find mush, you push. If you find steel, you withdraw." Vladimir Putin follows the same strategy. This week, as his forces shell Kyiv and batter Kharkiv, Putin has been upping the ante. He has unleashed strikes against Ukrainian targets near the Polish border, tacitly threatening to attack a NATO member. He continues to leverage his natural gas and oil supply to hold Europe hostage. His foreign policy apparatus continues to threaten the possibility of wider war should the West send in further armaments including MiGs sufficient to repel the Russian invasion. He has reached out to China for support. And he has utilized America's overweening desire for some sort of Iranian nuclear deal to press for American concessions on evading sanctions.

All of Putin's pressure has met with mixed response. The West has continued shipments of certain types of materiel, including Javelin and Stinger missiles. But this week, the Biden administration signaled first that it would allow shipment of MiGs to Ukraine, then backed off, claiming that such shipments might amount to escalation. Meanwhile, the West's economic sanctions are being maintained—but Russia announced this week that the United States had made written concessions that would exempt Russia's ability to trade with Iran, despite Iran firing missiles at a U.S. consulate in Erbil, Iraq.

What's the chief message from all of this waffling? That the West's threats are, at best, sporadically credible. Russia believes that if it ramps up the pressure harshly enough on Ukraine and threatens the West enough with nuclear war, it will be able to pry out of Ukraine diplomatically what it has been unable to pry out of Ukraine militarily—and Russia may well succeed. After all, Germans can't continue to pay $8.25 per gallon for gas forever.

At the same time, China, which has been playing both sides against the middle, is watching. China has been offering itself out as a "neutral mediator" between Russia and the West, despite the fact that China is an out-and-out Putin ally. China has been buying up troubled Russian assets at bargain-basement prices, strengthening both their connections with Russia and their portfolio—and meanwhile, China has received little credible threat of blowback from the West, which does not want to exacerbate inflationary problems by intensifying supply chain issues. As The New York Times reported, "a consensus is forming in Chinese policy circles that one country stands to emerge victorious from the turmoil: China." Investors are beginning to worry about the possibility of a Chinese invasion of Taiwan.

Nonaligned countries are increasingly skittish about Western promises. It is no coincidence that as Team Biden reaches out to Iran via Russia, Saudi Arabia has declined to take Biden's phone calls and instead reached out to China. It is no wonder that India, which buys exorbitant amounts of weaponry from Russia to counter China and Pakistan, has refused to denounce Russia. When the West wavers, it becomes a bad bet.

Western deterrence already failed in Ukraine. If the West fails to reestablish deterrence in the next phase of global geopolitics, the results will be even more dire, and the realignment currently playing out will only accelerate—to the detriment of the U.S. and her allies.

Should the West Seek an Off-Ramp in Ukraine?

October 5, 2022

How does the war in Ukraine end?

This is precisely the question no one is supposed to ask these days. The supposition by our thought leaders seems to be that if we keep up the pressure on Vladimir Putin in Ukraine, he'll fold and go home; his threats to use tactical nuclear weapons on the battlefield are nothing more than saber-rattling. He will then retrench on the domestic front, resolidify his power and continue throwing his prospective enemies from third-story windows.

Perhaps that's actually the best-case scenario. Because if President Joe Biden gets his wish—if Putin is indeed ousted from power in Russia—what would follow could easily be even worse than Putin: the Russian public remains highly supportive of aggressive foreign action to expand the "empire"; other than the military, there are no well-organized or powerful groups in Russia, and Putin does have an inner circle of possible successors who are, if anything, more anti-West even than he is. If none of those successors take the fore, the possibility of internecine warfare akin to Syria isn't totally out of the realm of possibility either—and that, in a country armed with a massive and aging nuclear arsenal.

Then there's the other possibility: that Putin is serious, and that if he sees his mission in Ukraine failing, he actually unleashes nuclear weapons. Most observers thought Putin was saber-rattling over his threats to invade Ukraine in the first place; underestimating Putin's aggressive radicalism now could be foolish. And there are no real plans to deal with Putin unleashing a nuke: while former CIA director David Petraeus has suggested that America would respond by "leading a NATO, a collective effort, that would take out every

Russian conventional force that we can see and identify on the battlefield in Ukraine and also in Crimea and every ship in the Black Sea," that could also lead Putin to escalate even further, perhaps even trying to directly threaten a civilian center in NATO territory with nuclear weapons.

In November 1939, the Soviet Union invaded Finland, attempting to install a puppet communist government; the West united in opposition to Soviet intervention, shipping weaponry to the Finns, who bravely stood against the forces of Stalin. The USSR lost at least 126,000 soldiers over the course of the three-and-a-half-month war but responded in the late going with a massive infusion of troops and a heavy offensive that drove the Finns back on their heels. Faced with the prospect of open war with the Western powers, Stalin signed the Moscow Peace Treaty in March 1940, with the Finns ceding 9% of their territory to Stalin.

Was the mutual stand-down the best solution? Should the West have pressed Stalin to the brink in Finland? Perhaps. But the West was facing down Stalin and Hitler simultaneously. Today, the threat isn't a second front from a powerful enemy, but the direct threat of nuclear weapons. Henry Kissinger has been publicly excoriated for suggesting that the off-ramp to this conflict will be territorial concessions by Ukraine to Russia—a repeat of the Moscow Peace Treaty. But he may be correct, particularly if the West is unwilling to bear the full economic and military cost of a larger war with Russia—as historian Niall Ferguson writes, "Thus far, the West have given Zelensky and his brave people enough military and economic support to avoid losing. We are not yet giving them enough to win—and the window for victory is not infinite." In the end, it may be that the least-bad scenario is about simply preventing the worst-case scenario.

Lies, Damned Lies, and Ukraine

July 12, 2023

As the Russian war in Ukraine drags on, three phrases have become a constant political drumbeat: "fight for democracy"; "as long as it takes"; and "until Ukraine wins." Each phrase is vague, bordering on incoherent; together, those phrases are leading the West down the primrose path to endless quagmire.

There are clear Western interests in Ukraine: prevention of Russian aggression across borders; degradation of the Russian military, so as to undercut future aggression; deterrence of China from taking similar action in Taiwan; and solidification of the European alliance against both Russia and China. The West has achieved virtually all of these goals: The chances that Kyiv falls to Moscow are now essentially zero.

Yet, the West, in maintaining that Ukrainian President Volodymyr Zelenskyy must lead all negotiations, has now boxed itself in. It does so on the basis, first, of the "fight for democracy." This is wrong on both practical and political levels. Practically, as mentioned, Ukrainian democracy is not likely to fall to Russia—and the greatest future threats to Ukrainian democracy will likely be internal corruption. Politically, no one believes that the West will maintain an open-ended war against Russia in order to preserve "democracy"—the West abandoned Afghanistan's nascent democracy after a 20-year effort to the tender predations of the Taliban.

The West has also said that it will maintain the war "as long as necessary." This, too, is a lie—and everyone, including Russia, knows it. After Iraq and Afghanistan, does anyone believe that the West will keep up funding to the tune of hundreds of billions of dollars?

Finally, the West says that Ukraine must "win." But by most

metrics, the West has *already* won. The West has little interest in toppling Putin—if, for example, the Wagner Group had taken over Russia, that would not have been a positive step in favor of world peace. And all of its original goals have been largely attained.

The question is what the West's interest are *now*. The West knows, for example, that this war will not end with all Russian troops leaving historic Ukrainian territory. Ukraine will not wind up in control of Crimea, or all of the Luhansk and Donetsk region; Ukraine's vaunted counteroffensive has made less progress than originally projected, because aggressive war is more difficult than defensive war. Yet the West continues to maintain that any end to this conflict must be negotiated by Zelenskyy, who has said that the war will not end until all Ukrainian territory is liberated of Russian presence.

So, what would an end to the war look like? Everyone has known the answer to this question for over a year: Ukraine preserves her sovereignty, and is given Western guarantees of defense, including possible membership in NATO; Russian control of Crimea and parts of Donbas is confirmed. Such a deal, imposed from the outside, would also give Zelenskyy an off-ramp with his own people: He'd be able to blame the West for forcing him to give away territory, which would allow him to retain his leadership position.

But that would be "our" definition of winning, which President Joe Biden and other Western leaders have specifically forbidden. So, we're now in the Catch-22 of saying that we'll support Zelenskyy's untenable "win everything" war and that we will also only admit Zelenskyy to NATO once the war has ended—creating an incentive for both Zelenskyy and Putin to continue the war. This is unnecessary. And it's happening due to the cowardice of Biden and other Western leaders, who want to look like heroes while simultaneously putting Zelenskyy and the West in an unwinnable quagmire of a situation.

Ukraine, Inner Cities, and Character Attacks

July 19, 2023

This weekend, Tucker Carlson interviewed a bevy of Republican presidential candidates in Iowa. Despite the fact that polls show that nearly zero Americans consider the war in Ukraine to be a top voting priority, Carlson spent a disproportionate share of his time grilling the candidates over their position on Ukraine. He took the position that favoring additional aid to Ukraine in its defensive war against Russia amounted to taking money out of the hands of poverty-stricken Americans in inner cities; as he asked Mike Pence, "Every city in the United States has become much worse over the past three years. Our economy has degraded. The suicide rate has jumped. Public filth and disorder and crime have exponentially increased. And yet your concern is that the Ukrainians, a country most people can't find on a map, who've received tens of billions of U.S. tax dollars, don't have enough tanks?"

This same line of logic was utilized over the weekend by Sen. J.D. Vance, R-Ohio, who spoke at the Turning Point USA conference in Florida. "There's no issue that these people with the Ukrainian flags in their bio are more obsessed with, they call it entitlement reform but what they're saying is they want to cut Social Security … so we can send more money to Volodymyr Zelenskyy in Ukraine," Vance said. Never mind the fact that this is patently untrue: Those with Ukraine flags in their Twitter bios are highly likely to favor massive governmental expenditures domestically. Never mind the fact that Vance himself used to be a proponent of entitlement reform.

The true concern is the absolutely specious link between a hawkish foreign policy and apathy about domestic concerns. Ukraine has become a litmus test not because many Americans care about it as a top issue; it has become a top issue because many commentators and politicians now make the argument that if you wish to spend a dollar in Ukraine to fend off Russian predation, you must be unconcerned about the suffering of American citizens here at home.

There are several problems with this logic.

First off, the basic notion that pouring government money into inner cities somehow cures them of their problems is belied by 60 years of trying just that strategy, to massive failure. In most cases, we'd be better off not spending government dollars on boondoggle programs, no matter where else we spend money.

Then there's the argument that isolationist foreign policy somehow results in greater American prosperity—that American citizens would be better off if we simply allowed Russia to march into Kyiv. This argument is disconnected from reality. It has no logical limits—why not let China take Taiwan or Russia take Poland? What's the limiting principle? But it also ignores the fact that American citizens have real interests abroad: The Ukraine war has disrupted supply lines in resources ranging from platinum and titanium to grain and oil; Russia's routine threats against its neighbors and expansionism in regions ranging from Africa to Syria threaten American allies and strengthen America's enemies, who further threaten American economic and security interests; China, buoyed by a soft Western response, would presumably move toward a full-scale Taiwan invasion.

Hawkishness is not allied to domestic poverty; in fact, hawkishness in the aftermath of World War II helped protect the safety of the oceans and the skies, thus leading to the greatest outpouring of prosperity in history. But regardless of what you think of America's support for Ukraine, it is dishonest to suggest that those who seek to fund Ukraine are universally apathetic about their fellow Americans. That implication is yet another symptom of our broken and polarized politics, in which nuanced arguments are ignored in favor of character attacks.

Putin Is Pushing Where There's Mush

February 21, 2024

This week, Vladimir Putin finally—allegedly—murdered his chief political rival and critic Alexei Navalny. Navalny's death followed an attempt by Putin's operatives in 2020 to kill him by poisoning; Navalny survived the attempt, worked with online specialists to unmask the actual agents responsible for the poisoning and then returned to Russia, where he was promptly arrested on trumped-up charges and sent to a Gulag in the far north.

Now, Navalny is dead.

And Putin isn't stopping there. This week, the Russian government announced an arrest warrant for Navalny's brother, Oleg, on unspecified charges; Putin's agents likely murdered a Russia defector to the Ukrainian side, who was found riddled with bullets in Spain; Putin's government arrested a Russian-American dual citizen on treason charges for giving some $50 to a group called Razom for Ukraine, which sends medical and hospital equipment to the beleaguered country.

Meanwhile, Putin is stepping up his international outreach efforts. This week, Putin invited the terror group Hamas to Moscow to talk, along with fellow terrorist leaders from Islamic Jihad and the Palestinian Authority. He also received plaudits from far-left corrupt Brazilian president Lula Da Silva, who refused to condemn Russia for Navalny's death but found time to accuse Israel of perpetrating a new Holocaust in the Gaza Strip. And, of course, last week he hosted Tucker Carlson for an interview, in which he laid out his historic grievances against NATO and Ukraine; Carlson then followed suit by issuing a series of videos praising Russian metro stations and supermarkets, claiming that Russian food prices should "radicalize" Americans into despising their leaders.

Putin feels unbound.

And he should.

Joe Biden is a weak leader with no centralizing principles. He has slow-walked aid to Ukraine since the beginning of the war; he has insisted on continued funding for the war while refusing to articulate what an end to the war would look like; he has refused to even justify the war to Americans beyond simply repeating the word "democracy" over and over—empty rhetoric that no longer tugs at the heartstrings in a complex world where the U.S. has non-democratic allies of its own. Biden refuses to take serious action on the southern border in order to achieve the Ukraine aid package he insists he desires; he even refuses to negotiate with the speaker of the House, Mike Johnson, on the issue. He seems to prefer tearing into Republicans for their insufficient zeal in funding Ukraine. All of this focus on Republicans allows Biden to elide the split in his own party—a split between Wilsonian interventionists and Noam Chomsky anti-Americans, who believe the United States to be a malevolent force in the world.

Meanwhile, Republicans are split, too. There are essentially four camps into which the Republican Party has split: neo-conservative interventionists, a remaining rump from the Bush years, who have historically supported nation-building efforts in far-flung regions with the goal of cultivating democratic allies even in inhospitable places; realpolitik devotees, who seek to assess each foreign conflict and all foreign aid with an eye toward hard American interests, ranging from the economic to the military; isolationists, who oppose all American interventions, both economic and military, on principle, believing that foreign policy generally represents a betrayal of priorities closer to home; and anti-Americans, who meet with the Chomsky-ite left in a perfect example of horseshoe theory made real.

Putin sees all of these splits. He sees the fact that Americans are distracted by domestic concerns, pried apart by competing narratives of the country, at each others' throats over everything from the definition of sex to the role of the government in everyday life—and split even on the question of whether America is a force for good or ill in the world.

Vladimir Lenin once supposedly said, "Probe with bayonets. If you find mush, you push. If you find steel, you withdraw."

Putin is probing. And he's finding nothing but mush.

The Cost of COVID

The Quest to Destroy Work

January 19, 2022

This week, after spending time vacationing in the disease-ridden hellscape known as Florida, Rep. Alexandria Ocasio-Cortez, D-N.Y., came down with COVID-19. It was a tragic blow to the irrepressible Instagram star, who was forced to quarantine. But then, like an extraordinarily inaniloquent phoenix rising from the ashes of the dread omicron variant, she returned to her web audience with a message for the ages.

"Welp, so it happened," she wrote, in truly Tolstoyan fashion. "Got COVID, probably omicron. As of today I am thankfully recovered and wrapping up quarantine, but COVID was no joke. For a while I've noted the term 'mild' is misleading when the bar is hospitalization and death." After dispensing with the preliminary medical advice, Ocasio-Cortez got down to business—or rather, to the business of avoiding doing business. She explained, "The idea of forcing people to work just 5 days after symptoms start is sociopathic and 100% informed by a culture that accepts sacrificing human lives for profit margins as a fair trade."

Now, this is, to put it mildly, dumb as a box of rocks. No one is suggesting that people with significant COVID-19 symptoms ought to go back to work. And nobody is sacrificing human lives by encouraging those with waning or no symptoms to return to the office. Businesses cannot run without employees.

Fortunately for us, the brilliant, "So Fresh, So Face" congresswoman has a solution: community. And by community, she means government. And by government, she means your money. "If you've noticed," she writes, "much of the emphasis on media conversations on COVID are individualistic—if there's one lesson I think we as a country are repeating until we learn, it's that community and collective good is our best shot through our greatest challenges—way more than discorded acts of 'rugged individualism' and the bootstrap propaganda we've been spoon-fed since birth ... In a world of MEs, let's build team WE. (Blue heart emoji)"

So, what exactly is the illustrious congresswoman proposing? Presumably, that businesses pay people to stay home if they are mildly symptomatic or asymptomatic; or that the government regulate businesses into such activity; or that taxpayers pay the freight. This accords with other proposals from Ocasio-Cortez, such as her Green New Deal idea to provide "economic security to all those who are unable or unwilling to work."

And Ocasio-Cortez's message is mirrored by even higher-level politicians like Speaker of the House Nancy Pelosi, who once proposed that Americans be provided nationalized health care so that they could leave their jobs en masse, thereby freeing them to "be a photographer or a writer or a musician, whatever, an artist." In the view of the far Left, work is a bad, foisted upon unwilling individuals by a cruel and arbitrary system. If only the system could be run properly, in top-down fashion by great minds like Ocasio-Cortez or Pelosi, Americans would be freed from the tyranny of everyday life.

Of course, precisely the opposite is true. Someone, as it turns out, has to pay the bills. And what's more, Americans generally *like* working. They find work fulfilling. Depression rates are twice as high among the unemployed than the employed—and more than three times as high for those unemployed for more than 27 weeks. Most Americans aren't eager to spend their days locked in their apartments waiting for government checks. And they're even less eager to spend more money at the store thanks to supply issues caused by lack of production due to labor shortages.

But Ocasio-Cortez and Pelosi don't have to worry about all of that. Ocasio-Cortez can always Instagram Live from her apartment or Zoom into congressional conference calls. And she never has to worry about the profit margins she spends so much time deriding; she can undercut those for others at her leisure.

Democrats used to pose as the party of labor. Now, they're increasingly the party of those who wish to avoid it at all costs.

The COVID-19 Impact of Expressive Individualism

January 26, 2022

Philosopher Robert Bellah once posited that modern Western human beings identify themselves in a peculiar way: as emotional cores, surrounded by baser material. According to Bellah, we are expressive individualists—meaning that "each person has a unique core of feeling and intuition that should unfold or be expressed if individuality is to be realized." This mode of self-definition wars with older, more traditional modes, which suggest that our identities lie in how we interact with the world and society around us. Expressive individualism, by contrast, suggests that we are not truly ourselves unless the world confirms all of our feelings and intuitions. As professor Carl Trueman points out, this viewpoint is essentially solipsistic; he explains, "When identity is psychologized, and the pursuit of happiness becomes a subjective, psychological matter, anything that challenges that paradigm is deemed damaging and oppressive."

We see this phenomenon most obviously in the bizarre insistence by transgender advocates that not only are they men trapped in women's bodies or vice versa, but that society mirror that incorrect self-perception. But expressive individualism also manifests in other contexts, such as belief in racial essentialism, denial of parental rights, and objection to science itself.

It even crops up in reference to COVID-19.

COVID-19 should be a paradigmatic example of where expressive individualism fails: It is an exogenous shock to the individual, a reality that exists no matter the subjective thoughts or feelings. The data map out individuals' risk factors; particular actions, like vaccination, can lower the risk of hospitalization or death for most people, no matter the intuitions of individuals who object. All of which mean that we should be able to track that data, and to change our response to the pandemic based on new data.

And yet we have now, as a society, psychologized even COVID-19 in expressive individualist terms. Thus, after Bari Weiss pointed out on Bill Maher's show that the public health establishment has failed time and again to follow the data, that the vast majority of those who have been vaccinated are safe from COVID-19, and that we ought to consider life returning to normal, a massive backlash ensued—backlash from those least vulnerable to COVID-19, who have now internalized a sense of COVID-19 moral superiority. Thus, Sara Haines of "The View" lamented, "I think some of the things we've learned in this pandemic will stay the same. I may never ride the subway without a mask, I may never go indoors to big crowds and feel comfortable without a mask." Michelle Goldberg of The New York Times explained, "What you can't do is force other people, whose vulnerabilities might be much greater than your own, to agree with your risk assessments and join you in moving on while the pandemic still rages."

But that's precisely what Goldberg and Haines are doing—forcing other people to take measures that the science does not support in order to maintain *their* emotional comfort. Boosters are not stopping omicron. Nothing short of N95 masks is stopping omicron. The disease is now endemic, which is why Dr. Hans Kluge of the World Health Organization's European region stated this week, "Omicron offers plausible hope for stabilization and normalization."

But there will be no normalization for those who have made pandemic paranoia a feature of their identity. That's because the public health establishment has now successfully cultivated a large group of people who measure their moral value by just how compliant and panicked they remain over COVID-19: Fully 68% of people fully vaccinated with boosters remain very or somewhat worried about getting sick from COVID-19 in the next year, compared with just 39% of those who are unvaccinated. This is the precise opposite of what the public health authorities should have achieved—but expressive individualism has won the day once again, conflating one's feelings with one's identity group.

Canada Goes Tyrannical

February 16, 2022

This week, Canadian Prime Minister Justin Trudeau, the lightweight, unpopular elected leader of a country with a 93% vaccination rate for those over 60 and a total vaccination rate of 84%, announced that he would invoke the Emergencies Act in order to crack down on the Freedom Convoy—a group of protesters opposed to government vaccination mandates for truckers. Trudeau breathily announced that invocation of the law was in fact "reasonable and proportionate." His public safety minister, Marco Mendicino, said that the actions were required thanks to "intimidation, harassment, and expressions of hate."

Why the government would need to invoke emergency powers in order to move some trucks remains beyond understanding; after all, the police had just removed trucks from the Ambassador Bridge, reopening that trade artery with the United States. Meanwhile, provinces across Canada have already begun alleviating their COVID-19 restrictions, from vaccine passports to masking. There is no emergency here that would justify use of the Emergencies Act— as even the BBC noted, "It is so far unclear which scenario Mr. Trudeau would rely on to justify the use of the Emergency Act—(the relevant threats have not) been clearly present in Ontario."

Nonetheless, Finance Minister Chrystia Freeland explained that the government would be extending laws designed to stop terror funding to now encompass crackdowns on political dissent: "Financial service providers will be able to immediately freeze or suspend an account without a court order. In doing so, they will be protected against civil liability for actions taken in good faith." In plain language, this means that the government of Canada has now empowered banks to freeze accounts who give money to political causes the government doesn't like.

The move to de-bank disfavored political actors has already been gaining steam—in January 2021, PayPal blocked a Christian crowdfunding site from using its services; the next month, Paypal announced it would work with the Left-wing Southern Poverty Law Center to find users to boot. As one of Paypal's original creators, David Sacks, wrote, "when your name lands on a No-Buy List created by a consortium of private fintech companies, to whom can you appeal?" In Canada, it's worse than that: The de-banking has become government sponsored.

And if Trudeau is able to invoke emergency powers to de-bank his political opponents—people he has labeled racists simply for opposing his vaccine mandates—where, precisely, does this end? What's to stop powerful political actors from violating liberties on the same pretext?

The answer, of course, is nothing. And perhaps that's the point: from now on, dissent against Left-wing perspectives may be criminalized. Watch what you say—your bank account is on the line.

Over the course of the past century, the political Left made a promise: that if they were granted more and more centralized power, they would protect their citizens, particularly during times of emergency. That promise was always a lie, but the pandemic exploded that lie in particularly egregious fashion. This left the Left with two options: to abandon that article of faith, an idea central to their entire worldview; or to persecute heretics. Trudeau, unsurprisingly, has chosen the latter. Emergency powers will be necessary until the people enthusiastically agree that their betters in government ought to rule them.

The COVID-19 Authoritarians Panic over the End of the Mask Mandates

April 20, 2022

This week, a federal judge in Florida finally struck down a federal mask mandate from the Centers for Disease Control and Prevention. An extensive number of executive branch agencies have acted in an authoritarian manner throughout the COVID-19 era: The Occupational Safety and Health Administration infamously attempted to cram down a vaccine mandate on every private employer in America, a policy struck down by the Supreme Court; the CDC blocked evictions for over a year based on the premise that millions would be thrown from their homes if they didn't take action. But the CDC's travel mask mandate has been particularly annoying for Americans, given the fact that all over the country, Americans have either been vaccinated or acquired natural immunity, and there is no evidence whatsoever that cloth or surgical masks do anything against the omicron variant of COVID-19.

Nonetheless, the CDC pressed forward this month with a new extension to its mask mandate, despite the fact that the CDC simultaneously argued that beginning in late May, it would relieve Title 42, a regulation designed to allow Border Patrol to turn away likely illegal immigrants at the border. That regulation was rooted in the premise that a COVID-19 emergency negated the legal requirement to process asylum seekers. The White House provided zero justification for the CDC's extension; instead, White House press secretary Jen Psaki struggled to explain why toddlers on planes should remain masked, but attendees at the White House press room didn't have to. "I'm not a doctor," she spat.

Of course, Psaki's lack of medical background hasn't prevented her from announcing that the best standard of medical care requires minors who are gender confused to receive puberty blockers on the path toward genital-mutilating surgery. But Americans shouldn't expect consistency from their moral betters in the White House.

Upon the announcement of the judge's ruling striking down the CDC mask mandate on the grounds that the CDC hadn't actually bothered to follow its own regulatory procedures, the Left went into spasms of apoplexy. Public figures began posting pictures of themselves donning masks on planes: former Obama senior adviser Valerie Jarrett tweeted, "Wearing my mask no matter what non-scientists tell me I can do"; Roland Martin tweeted, "I don't give a damn what some grossly unqualified Donald Trump judge said. I'm double masked and wearing goggles on this Nashville to DC flight. I had COVID in December. Y'all can KISS MY ASS about me not wanting it again. And any fool saying they don't matter is a damn liar."

Now, it should be said that nobody has actively *banned anyone from wearing a mask*. It is your choice to don one, as epidemiologically useless as such a gesture may be. But those on the Left seem to be under the wild misimpression that anything not prohibited is now mandatory—an act of pure intellectual projection springing from the Left's insistence on collective rulemaking. For those on the Left, individual freedom represents a threat to everyone; to allow individuals the ability to choose therefore undermines the entire scheme. Those on the Left simply project this mindset onto everyone else. Thus, they believe that anyone who opposes mask mandates wants to force everyone to unmask.

This is untenable but predictable: for those on the Left, the collective is the irreducible unit of politics. There are no individuals. And anyone who disagrees is, in the words of Robin Givhan of The Washington Post, "childish and selfish."

Or perhaps—just perhaps—the most childish and selfish among us are those who beg government agencies to exceed their statutory authority in order to ensure that we all mirror their favored priorities. Perhaps those who have spent two years declaring their authority over every aspect of Americans' lives ought to consider the possibility that we're happy to let them ruin their own, but that we would prefer they leave us alone. And most of all, perhaps the COVID-19 paranoiacs ought to spend just a moment considering whether there is a space between mandatory and prohibited where others might be granted a smidgen of liberty.

The Greatest Cover-Up in Human History

March 1, 2023

First, it was supposedly a conspiracy theory.

Then, it was banned.

Finally, it was true.

The so-called "lab leak" theory of the origins of COVID-19—the theory that COVID-19 originated in at the Wuhan Institute of Virology and then was unintentionally loosed—was always the most probable explanation for the outbreak of the deadly virus. After all, as Jon Stewart correctly joked in 2021, "'Oh, my God, there's a novel respiratory coronavirus overtaking Wuhan, China. What do we do?' 'Oh, you know who we could ask? The Wuhan novel respiratory coronavirus lab.' The disease is the same name as the lab. That's just a little too weird, don't you think?"

But for well over a year, it was considered verboten to mention the lab leak theory. When Senator Tom Cotton, R-Ark., posited the possibility of a lab leak in February 2020, he was roundly mocked by the media. The New York Times headlined, "Senator Tom Cotton Repeats Fringe Theory of Coronavirus Origins." Scientific American headlined—in March 2022!—"The Lab-Leak Hypothesis Made It Harder for Scientists to Seek the Truth." Facebook actively quashed attempts to disseminate the theory; Dr. Anthony Fauci went on national television and downplayed the theory.

Why?

Two reasons are obvious. The first: powerful institutions had a stake in downplaying the Chinese origins of the virus in order to shift blame to the rest of the world. Certainly, that was China's game: In all likelihood, COVID-19 was spreading in China as early as October 2019, and the government covered it up for months. But that was also the game of the World Health Organization. Members of the American government like Fauci also had a stake in smothering questions about American funding for gain-of-function research in Wuhan.

Then there's the second reason: all the wrong people were repeating the lab leak theory. As one of MSNBC's resident hacks, Mehdi Hasan, admitted on Twitter, "The simple reason why so many people weren't keen to discuss the 'lab leak' theory is because it was originally conflated by the right with 'Chinese bio weapon' conspiracies and continues to be conflated by the right with anti-Fauci conspiracies. Blame the conspiracy theorists." As Nate Silver correctly noted, "The Bad People thought the lab leak might be true, therefore as journalists we couldn't be expected to actually evaluate the evidence for it."

Herein lies a lesson: A huge number of people have decided that there are a cadre of people who are so vile that any opinion they touch is immediately toxified beyond investigation. Claims are not to be evaluated on their own merits; instead, we can simply determine whether a claim ought to be supported based on those who posit it. This helps to explain why political crossover has become nearly impossible: We're not judging the claims of our opponents; we're judging *each* other. And this means that we can discard any argument simply by dint of the fact that we don't like the person offering it.

Among members of the general population, this is a problem, but not a fundamental one. But among those who pose as "experts"—the people who are supposed to serve as guides for people who outsource their political information, from media to scientific institutions—it's a fatal error. After all, experts are supposed to be impartial adjudicators of the evidence. That's their entire job. We can evaluate on our own who we don't like—but we often need help to determine whether an argument has merit or not. When experts become "just like us," they undermine their raison d'etre.

And that's precisely what happened with COVID-19. Whether it was ignoring the actual evidence regarding masks and mask mandates, the evidence regarding post-vaccination transmissibility or the evidence regarding the lab leak theory, experts decided that the *wrong people* had to be ignored. But they were wrong. And now they have no credibility left.

There Is No Short Path Back to Institutional Credibility

June 21, 2023

Institutional trust is built over the course of years. Decades. Centuries.

Dishonesty takes just a moment to destroy institutional trust.

This week, Dr. Peter Hotez, dean of the National School of Tropical Medicine and professor of molecular virology at Baylor College of Medicine, got into a spat with podcaster Joe Rogan and presidential candidate Robert F. Kennedy Jr. Hotez has a long-standing feud over vaccine efficacy and safety with RFK Jr., who has long been a proponent of the scientifically unverified theory that childhood vaccines cause autism; RFK Jr., appearing on Rogan's podcast, tore into Hotez. Hotez responded by accusing Rogan of spreading "misinformation"—to which Rogan quite properly responded that if Hotez wished to rebut that "misinformation" in debate with RFK Jr. on his show, he'd be happy not only to host but to contribute $100,000 to a charity of Hotez's choice. Hotez refused the invite. He then appeared on MSNBC, where he explained, "Anti-vaccine disinformation … is now a lethal force in the United States. I offered to go on Joe Rogan but not to turn it into the Jerry Springer show with having RFK Jr. on."

This is still a free country; no one is obligated to debate anyone else. But Hotez essentially argues that his credentials excuse him from having to defend his case publicly in debate. In the past, there might have been something to that: Few would have expected a virologist to debate, say, Jenny McCarthy, even 20 years ago, for better or worse. Why? Because the scientific community could point to decades of success in health outcomes—longer, healthier lives and fewer childhood diseases among them. The scientists acted *as scientists,* predominantly worried about following evidence and producing functional solutions to human problems.

Then the scientists decided to promote garbage while hiding behind their credentials. They claimed that men could be women; that universal masking would stop the spread of COVID-19; that schools had to be closed to stop mass death from COVID-19 among children, and that at the same time, protesters on behalf of "racial justice" could safely congregate in close proximity; that the COVID-19 vaccine would stop transmission; that capitalism had to be curbed to stop global warming. They used the credibility of science to preach political nonsense.

And in just a few years, the credibility gained by our scientific institutions has completely eroded. Just 41% of Americans now say that they believe the Centers for Disease Control are doing an excellent or good job. That distrust is entirely earned, given the CDC's egregiously awful performance during the COVID-19 pandemic.

All of this means that those who purport to speak in the name of science—the same people who have used that label to avoid debate—must now wade back into the arena. They simply don't have the credibility to demand the trust of the public. It's time to earn it.

Social Issues

The War On Parents Continues

February 23, 2022

In September 2020, January Littlejohn went to pick up her 13-year-old daughter from middle school. Littlejohn is a stay-at-home mother to three children and a licensed mental health counselor in Florida. So when her daughter informed her that the school administration had begun encouraging her to identify as transgender, Littlejohn was shocked.

Littlejohn's daughter told her that school administrators had asked her about changing her name, which restroom she wished to use, and whether she wanted to sleep with boys or girls on school trips. According to the district, parents were to be cut out of the loop unless the 13-year-old gave her consent to their involvement; the district stated that "outing a student, especially to parents, can be very dangerous to the student's health and well-being."

So, to be clear, the school would have had to phone Littlejohn for permission to administer an Advil; presumably if Littlejohn's daughter had been suffering from depression or anxiety in school, parents would have been notified as well. But the school purposefully avoided telling Littlejohn about her daughter considering whether she was a boy or a girl, and all the attendant acts toward social transition—all of which is often followed by hormone replacement or surgery. The school not only felt no duty to keep Littlejohn in the loop, but they also treated Littlejohn as an enemy to her own child.

This, indeed, is the mentality of an enormous swath of the social Left these days. Florida is now considering a bill, the Parental Rights in Education bill, that would restrict primary schools from indoctrinating children on matters of sexual orientation or gender identity and would require schools to inform parents about minors who begin identifying as LGBTQ in school. None of this should be controversial: Parents have always been and will always be the adults with the most stake in their children. It is parents who care most about their children, not school administrators; it is parents who shape the values and choices of their children.

But that's precisely what the Left hates. To the Left, parents are the enemy. Without any evidence of abuse—or even any allegations of abuse—the Left now states that forcing schools to provide transparency to parents about their children is a form of abuse. As California Gov. Gavin Newsom put it, telling schools to keep parents in the loop is "nothing short of a state-sponsored intimidation of LGBTQ children. It will put kids—who are already navigating stress—in physical and psychological danger."

The Left, instead, wishes to teach its own version of sexual morality and gender identity to small children, without the messy intervention of parents. It is indeed that simple. And, of course, this has an impact. It is designed to have an impact. There is a reason that, according to Gallup, just 0.8% of those born before 1946 identify as LGBT, and that just 2.6% of those born between 1946 and 1964 do—but that fully 20.8% of all those born between 1997 and 2003 identify as LGBT. That reason is not evolutionary biology making a radical turn, or even additional tolerance for such activity. The reason is that our society has decided that belief in traditional standards with regard to both sex and sexual activity must be fought tooth and nail. Any parent who holds to those standards must be treated as a threat—not to the children they care about far more than activists do, but to the new standard.

Now, perhaps the new standard is somehow superior to the old. If the Left wishes to make that case, they can certainly do so. But the Left does not have the right to hijack the minds of children and then weaponize them against their parents using public dollars, all the while pretending that such activity is actually altruism on behalf of children. It isn't. It's cruel to children and cruel to parents.

It's Time for the Market Pushback to Begin

March 23, 2022

This week, The Walt Disney Company, which has approximately 200,000 employees spanning the globe, decided to radically reshape its politics in response to a tiny contingent of radical activists. According to The Wall Street Journal, Disney CEO Bob Chapek had steadfastly refused to embroil his company in the politics of the various states and countries where Disney did business; he correctly noted that the job of the company was to continue to make magic, not to do the political bidding of any favored coterie.

Then, the state of Florida passed a law that would ban the indoctrination of small children into left-wing perspectives regarding gender identity and sexual orientation. And all hell broke loose. Senior Disney executives began circulating letters stating that the company opposed the Florida legislation, which opponents had falsely labeled the "Don't Say Gay" bill (the bill doesn't mention the word gay once). And some employees threatened a walkout if Disney did not reorient itself toward their favored political position.

So Chapek caved. He sent a letter to staff stating, "You needed me to be a stronger ally in the fight for equal rights and I let you down. I am sorry." He then pledged a listening tour, the formation of a task force to cater to LGBT priorities, and opposition to a Texas measure that would prosecute genital mutilation or hormonal sterilization of children. The company also committed itself to injecting its radical left-wing values in content, including "new content for children and family" infused with those values. According to reports, Disney even went so far as to commit to including a lesbian kiss in its upcoming children's film "Lightyear."

Chapek is caving because this is what left-leaning corporations do: they listen to their most outraged left-wing contingent, and then parrot them. Instead of giving an answer proper to an employer besieged by employees threatening a walkout—telling the employees to get back to work or join the unemployment lines— major companies simply surrender. Meanwhile, parents who simply wish their children to be entertained without being indoctrinated watch in perplexed horror as radical activists design content for their children.

In order to combat this nonsense, those who oppose the hijacking of major companies by the Left must get organized—and they must create alternatives. That's what we've tried to do at The Daily Wire. In 2021, Harry's Razors withdrew their advertising on one of our shows, citing a "values misalignment." What precisely was the problem? Our host had stated that men are men and women are women, and that sex is immutable.

So, we fought back. This week, we launched Jeremy's Razors, a razor company dedicated to the proposition that everyone, regardless of politics, deserves a good shave. We are here to provide you excellent products for you to use. And we will never slap our customers in the face thanks to the priorities of a woke few. That's why our motto is simple: "Shut up and shave."

If corporations decide to go woke, there must be competitors who assure that they will go broke. And we hope to fill that gap. We only hope others will follow our lead.

The Left Is the Culture War Aggressor

April 6, 2022

Last week, reporter Christopher Rufo released footage of top Disney employees vowing to inject their radical LGBTQ agenda into children's programming. Disney producer Latoya Raveneau told an all-hands meeting that her team works to push a "not-at-all-secret gay agenda" in programming aimed at kids and sought to add "queerness" to such content. Disney corporate president Karey Burke announced that she was the mother of "one transgender child and one pansexual child" and that she would try to achieve a quota system whereby half of all Disney characters would be LGBTQ or people of color. Disney diversity and inclusion manager Vivian Ware stated that Disney's beloved theme parks would be eliminating any mention of "ladies and gentlemen" or "boys and girls."

This prompted a well-deserved firestorm for the Mouse House. Disney has long been Left-wing on social issues—but in the aftermath of ginned-up controversy surrounding Florida's Parental Rights in Education bill, which protects small children from indoctrination on sexual orientation and gender identity, an angry coterie of employees pushed management to signal fealty even harder. So Disney's brass did, announcing that they opposed the Florida bill and then turning over the company to its most radical contingent.

And people reacted. #BoycottDisney began to trend on social media. We at the Daily Wire committed to spending $100 million to develop children's content that would be safe for kids—content dedicated to traditional values, where parents wouldn't have to worry about prescreening content for messages about nonbinary 5-year-olds.

The Left, caught with its hand in the kiddie jar, immediately swiveled and accused the Right of initiating this culture war.

Michelle Goldberg of The New York Times lamented that she felt terrible for Raveneau, who, after all, was just "step(ping) up to defend the company's queer friendliness, only to become a national object of right-wing fury and disgust," and whose injection of LGBTQ propaganda into children's content was "sweetly anodyne." CNN hosted Washington Post transgender columnist Charlotte Clymer, adding the chyron "LGBT COMMUNITY LATEST TO BE CAUGHT IN CULTURE WAR." The takeaway, according to the social Left, is that anyone who defends traditionalism in child-rearing—or anyone who simply doesn't want children turned into targets of sexual propagandizing—is the true cultural aggressor.

This is a transparent lie. And it's a lie that won't redound to the benefit of those who seek radical change. If they wish to pose the rubric of gay rights against parental rights, gay rights are likely to suffer. If they wish to suggest that LGBTQ freedom extends to teachers initiating children into sexual conversations without parental permission, parents are unlikely to go along for the ride. For decades, the social Left has made inroads by arguing that they simply want to be left alone. The Right, by contrast, has argued that the Left's agenda is far broader, that the Left demands cultural celebration of its sexual mores and that it will stop at nothing to remake society in order to achieve its narcissistic goals. Disney's latest foray into the culture wars proves that the Right was correct, that the Left's stated agenda was a lie and that its "not-at-all-secret" agenda targeted the most vulnerable Americans.

Disney shows no signs of backing away from the extremism its all-hands meeting unmasked before the world. And other corporations are following Disney's lead, pushing wild Left advocacy instead of catering to the broadest possible market. For too long, Americans have planted their heads firmly in the sand, hoping that the forces of the free market would militate against the cultural hijacking of corporate institutions. Instead, corporations built by entrepreneurs have been hijacked by woke employees and a feckless managerial class. The blowback will be real, and it should be real. And if that means parents swearing off Mickey Mouse, increasingly they will.

The End of the Road for Roe?

May 4, 2022

This week, an anonymous leaker violated generations of Supreme Court norms by passing on to Politico a draft decision by Justice Samuel Alito in Dobbs v. Mississippi, the case considering overturning Roe v. Wade (1973). That draft decision, reportedly supported by a majority of the Court including Justices Clarence Thomas, Neil Gorsuch, Brett Kavanaugh and Amy Coney Barrett, junks Roe in its entirety, denying the existence of any constitutional "right to abortion"; the majority opinion also trashes Roe's follow-up case, Planned Parenthood v. Casey (1992), which substituted a vague and unworkable "undue burden" test to determine whether or not a law restricting abortion was unconstitutional in place of Roe's trimester framework. Alito writes, "The Constitution does not prohibit the citizens of each State from regulating or prohibiting abortion. Roe and Casey arrogated that authority."

Alito is, of course, correct. Roe is a legal abomination with no support in the Constitution's text, our nation's history or any legal precedent. The Supreme Court merely usurped power in order to jam down its political opinions on millions of Americans; Roe didn't end national controversy on abortion, it froze it in place, preventing states from adopting regulations tailored to their voters. Overturning Roe would merely restore the question of abortion to the states; New York would continue to allow abortion until birth, while Texas would ban nearly all abortion.

But according to the Left, the end of Roe will usher in a fascistic hellscape. President Joe Biden called the decision "radical," and said, "The idea that we're letting the states make those decisions, localities make those decisions, would be a fundamental shift in what we've done." Senate Majority Leader Chuck Schumer called the decision a "dark and disturbing day for America," even as

Democrats called for attempting to nuke the filibuster to codify Roe into federal law. Sen. Elizabeth Warren, D-Mass., said she was "angry and upset ... The Republicans have been working toward this day for decades. They have been out there plotting, carefully cultivating these Supreme Court justices so they could have a majority on the bench who would accomplish something that the majority of Americans do not want."

Naturally, Warren was unwilling to explain why, if so many Americans support her point of view, she is opposed to allowing them to vote on the issue. But the answer is clear—as clear as the reason why the Left is perfectly sanguine about someone leaking the draft decision in the first place: Democratic norms, the Constitution, and principle are of no consequence. All that matters is result. The Left has viewed the Supreme Court as a preserve for progressive policymaking for decades. The Dobbs v. Mississippi decision would restore the Court to its original role: an impartial arbiter of the law, rather than a Left-wing superlegislature. And the Left cannot abide that possibility. They would prefer a Supreme Court that imposes Leftist social priorities from above.

That is particularly true when it comes to abortion, the most vital Leftist sacrament, an action of holy import. For the Left, abortion represents the power to deny the objective value of human life; it represents willingness to engage in the highest form of self-serving moral relativism. Absence of abortion presents the possibility that actions have moral consequence, that the value of life is not an arbitrary and subjective one, that women and men have duties to their children. All of which challenges their basic worldview. To have that logic subjected to the voters is an indignity the Left cannot bear. And they will use every tool in their arsenal to prevent that possibility.

For the Left, Children Are Either
Obstacles or Tools

May 11, 2022

In the aftermath of a leaked Supreme Court draft majority decision prospectively overruling Roe v. Wade, the Left in the United States has gone into full-fledged panic mode. That outsized panic has manifested as a variety of unconvincing or blatantly immoral arguments: the argument that abortion is a necessary adjunct to women's freedom—as though contraception doesn't exist, and as though women are never responsible for their own sexual decisions and the consequences thereof; the argument that unless society provides for any number of government programs, abortion should not be prohibited—as though the solution to lack of universal child care is the death of the child; the argument that conservatives will next attempt to outlaw interracial marriage—an absurd slander on its face.

Underlying all of this is a perverse and inverted view of children's role in society. To the Left, children in the womb are utterly disposable; at best, women *may* choose to preserve their lives, but if not, they have no separate interests to be considered. In fact, children are to be treated as potential obstacles: as Treasury Secretary Janet Yellen said this week, "access to reproductive health care, including abortion, helped lead to increased labor force participation; it enabled many women to finish school. That increased their earning potential." This explains why the Left has now embraced the language of "forced birth" to describe laws protecting the unborn: pregnancy is no longer seen as the possible biological outgrowth of sexual activity, but as a dramatic foreign imposition on women. The default, for the Left, is childlessness; pregnancy is somehow unnatural. Thus, the entire Democratic Party apparatus now refuses to countenance even the mildest restrictions on even late-term abortion.

Once children are born, the Left then sees them as sources of grief and pain for their parents. This, too, cuts in favor of abortion. As former President Barack Obama once stated about his daughters, "if they make a mistake, I don't want them punished with a baby." Babies are life-sucking entities, depriving women of opportunity and freedom. Which explains why the Left has now embraced the argument that unless government somehow relieves parents of their responsibility to raise and care for their own children, abortion ought to be broadly available.

As children grow, the Left sees them as the center of recruitment efforts on behalf of their favored politics. Children should be indoctrinated in the ideas of racial essentialism and historic guilt, so as to turn them into political widgets on behalf of utopian social change; children should be confused about the nature of biological sex and gender, so as to justify the sexual attitudes of narcissistic adults. Hence the Left's outsized rage at Florida's Parental Rights in Education bill, which merely banned sexual orientation and gender theory indoctrination for children through third grade. As the San Francisco Gay Men's Chorus sang in 2021, "You think that we'll corrupt your kids, if our agenda goes unchecked. Funny, just this once, you're correct. We'll convert your children. Happens bit by bit." No wonder President Joe Biden told teachers two weeks ago, "They're all our children … They're not somebody else's children, they're like yours when they're in the classroom."

All of this is fundamentally indecent. Adulthood lies in one primary task: protecting and defending children. This means bearing children is a gift, not an obstacle; this means that children should not be treated as autonomous adults while adults escape responsibility for their own decisions. This means raising children in line with values that ensure their stability and happiness—even if that means a tougher life for adults. All of that begins with a basic supposition the Left refuses to countenance: that they are not the center of creation, but that their children ought to be.

The Elitists Who Want to Rule the World

May 25, 2022

Klaus Schwab is the head of the World Economic Forum; he founded the organization in 1971. Each year, the WEF hosts a massive conference in Davos, Switzerland, with thousands of world leaders, diplomats and experts on various topics gathering to trade ideas about how best to cooperatively run the world. Lest this characterization be seen as overstating the case, Schwab himself said as much this year in opening the conference: "The future is not just happening. The future is built by us, by a powerful community as you here in this room. We have the means to improve the state of the world. But two conditions are necessary. The first one is that we act all as stakeholders of larger communities, that we serve not only self-interest but we serve the community. That's what we call stakeholder responsibility. And second, that we collaborate."

This is the call to action for elitists the world over. They appoint themselves the representatives of global interests—without elections, without accountability—and then create mechanisms of national and international order to control citizens over whom they claim to preside. Schwab himself has decoded his favorite term, "stakeholder capitalism." He wrote in Time magazine in October 2020, "Free markets, trade and competition create so much wealth that in theory they could make everyone better off if there was the will to do so." To do so, however, would require taking hints from Greta Thunberg, #MeToo and Black Lives Matter; it would require "building ... a virtuous economic system" in which companies abandon their core mission of serving customers and shareholders and instead embrace answering questions like "What is the gender pay gap in company X? How many people of diverse backgrounds were hired and promoted? What progress has the company made toward reducing its greenhouse-gas emissions?"

All of this extraordinary arrogance is predicated on a perverse view of how successful change works within decentralized systems. As Schwab himself acknowledges, free markets have generated more prosperity than any system in human history. But that's because free markets are *not* a top-down imposition, a system created by conspiratorial muckety-mucks in a back room somewhere. Free markets were the outgrowth of centuries of evolutionary societal progress: gradual recognition that private ownership was the greatest incentive toward work and innovation; incremental understanding that individual rights are the only alternative to endless conflict; step-by-step acceptance that decentralized sources of knowledge are both broader and deeper than centralized ones. The most powerful and durable institutions we have are traditional because, as F.A. Hayek wrote, they are "a product of cumulative growth without ever having been designed by any one mind."

For Schwab and his ilk, however, it's precisely such an evolutionary approach that must be ended. Instead, he and his rationalist buddies—brilliant businessmen and ambitious politicians, striving bureaucrats and myopic experts—will cure the world of its ills, so long as we grant them power. Or, more likely, so long as they seize power in the name of "stakeholders" to whom they are never answerable.

One of the great ironies of the past several years is the gap between the elitists' perception of themselves. To the elitists, their solutions failed because citizens of the world lacked the will to listen to them; to the citizens, the elitists failed because their prescriptions were ill-founded. Yet so long as the elitists retain their power, they will continue to push forward their utopian dreams at the expense of those they purport to serve.

The Anarchic Philosophy Behind 'LGBTQI+ Pride Month'

June 1, 2022

June marks LGBTQI+ Pride Month—a month honoring those who are "lesbian, gay, bisexual, transgender, queer and intersex." This ever-expanding rubric revolves around a particular value system entirely embraced by the modern Left: the notion that a person's core identity ought to lie not in the relationship between individual desires and societal duties, but instead ought to revolve around a subjective sense of self, unverifiable by the world at large and justified against all societal roles and rules.

President Joe Biden has said as much from the White House. In a proclamation urging Americans to "wave their flags of pride high"— it is worth noting that an entire side of the political aisle in the United States now finds the so-called pride flag far less controversial than the American flag itself—Biden stated, "This month, we remind the LGBTQI+ community that they are loved and cherished. My administration sees you for who you are—deserving of dignity, respect and support."

Of course, seeing people for who they are typically requires some sort of objective standard; it is literally impossible to see someone for who he is based on his own internal self-perception. This means that Biden is using perfectly Orwellian euphemisms to say that we all ought to validate the self-perception of any he, she, xe or catself.

This perspective is absolutely incoherent. Ironically, this incoherence is exposed by the conflict between the different letters within the alphabet soup of the supposedly sexually marginalized. The case for tolerance of lesbian and gay Americans used to be that biological drives should not be regulated by society at large, because such drives were inborn and innate; that idea at least had the merit of internal consistency. Now, however, that idea has been jettisoned for its logical opposite, the belief that biology has no hold on us whatsoever, and that we ought to be free to define ourselves in opposition to our own biology, changing our gender and sexual orientation at will. Homosexual orientation relies on the continued distinction between the sexes—after all, why prefer males or females if those sexes are mere social constructs? Transgenderism relies on the absolute malleability of sex. This is the reason that so-called TERFs—"trans-exclusionary radical feminists"—are so bewildered by the suddenly mainstream view that women's rights ought to be extended to biological men.

And yet here we are, told by the White House that we must ignore the internal contradictions of Left-wing sexual ideology, and simply pretend the incoherence away. We are told that we ought to stand for women's rights by the same people who insist that Lia Thomas is a woman; we are told that one need not be a biological female to be a lesbian; we are told that biology dictates behavior, but that biology must never be used as an identifier. None of this makes one whit of sense. But we ought to be proud of it, because after all, it liberates us to celebrate our inner sense of authenticity, free of society's strictures.

There is only one problem, of course: this sort of illogic quickly devolves into anarchy. There is no way to speak coherently with one another absent objective meaning, let alone to reach consensus. Suggesting that the world at large owes each of us validation for our innermost desires is a recipe for complete chaos. Unity can only come from opposition to something—and in this case, that means opposition to tradition, institutions and the roles that actually facilitate human flourishing.

Is Ignoring The Other Side A Winning Strategy For The Left?

June 8, 2022

This week, my company, The Daily Wire, premiered a blockbuster new documentary starring Matt Walsh. Titled "What Is A Woman?", the documentary investigates radical gender theory and its peculiar hold on the elites in our society—and how the insane proposition that men can become women and vice versa has become so well-accepted that even normal Americans now live in fear of questioning it. The film has been the single largest success in the history of The Daily Wire; hundreds of thousands of Americans have subscribed to view it. Yet Rotten Tomatoes, the review aggregator for film and television, has not a single traditional review of the film.

That's because, according to the legacy and entertainment media, the film doesn't exist. When the Daily Wire press team sent out invitations to reviewers to watch the film—knowing, of course, that the vast majority of reviewers are Left-leaning and would undoubtedly pan the film—reviewers began responding with insults and declarations of preemptive hatred. "Hard pass," wrote one. "Unsubscribe," wrote another. "Lose my email. Forget my name." A third reviewer, this one a member of GALECA: The Society of LGBTQ Entertainment Critics, wrote, "Hard f—ing pass. I won't give that transphobic bigot a platform on my site. Never email me again!" Thus, the current Rotten Tomatoes audience score for the film is 96%; the reviewer score remains empty.

Reviewers' willingness to pretend that there is no controversy with regard to gender and sex perfectly reflects the Left's beliefs about transgender ideology more broadly. One gender reassignment surgeon—a medical doctor who performs body-mutilating surgeries—told Walsh that nobody believed in traditional ideas about biological sex anymore; only "dinosaurs" would believe such antiquated notions.

Such denial of the mere existence of a countervailing argument is a common feature of the Left these days. The idea is that by pretending opposition to bizarre ideas doesn't exist, you can mainstream those bizarre ideas. Thus, "everyone believes" that climate change is not merely a byproduct of human activity, but that it threatens life on earth; to deny the latter proposition is tantamount to Holocaust denial. "Everyone believes" that America is systemically racist; to do otherwise is to mark yourself as a bigot.

But what if everybody *doesn't* believe such propositions? What if there are millions of Americans—the majority of Americans, in fact—who believe precisely the opposite? Then the only option is to reinforce denial with censorship. Which is why former Barack Obama senior adviser Dan Pfeiffer went on the air at MSNBC to declare the very popularity of conservative viewpoints a threat to democracy. "Right wing content," Pfeiffer observed, "dwarfs progressive content (on Facebook). It dwarfs mainstream media content, which actually should be the part that scares us the most, that Ben Shapiro's Daily Wire has more followers and engagement, many times more than The New York Times or CNN … That is a problem for democracy."

Democracy, you see, simply means the Approved View. If the Approved View is somehow unpopular, that must be a problem of propaganda, which is in turn a problem for democracy. The only solution is to ban such propaganda, thus leaving a monopoly on behalf of the Approved View. If the echo chamber isn't strong enough to drown out the outsiders, simply silence those outside the chamber, then declare democracy safe.

There's only one problem: it won't work. Democrats have siloed themselves into an increasingly progressive universe, one in which the most controversial imaginable propositions are utterly uncontroversial. In this universe, the other side doesn't exist. Unfortunately for the Left, the other side *does* exist. And they vote. And come November 2022, the ostrich strategy of the Democratic Party and its media apparatchiks is likely to bear devastating electoral fruit.

The Death of The Elite 'Center'

June 22, 2022

The false center cannot hold.

In France, President Emmanuel Macron has now lost his majority in the National Assembly; his party holds 245 seats in the lower house, but the Right holds 150 and the Left 131. In Colombia, former M-19 guerrilla and Marxist Gustavo Petro has now become the president of the country, replacing more establishment, Keynesian liberal rule. In the United States, the supposed center within both parties has been increasingly supplanted by anti-establishment forces on both sides.

None of this should be shocking, given the destruction of institutional trust throughout the West. And the destruction of that institutional trust has been well earned: It represents the natural result of policy elites lying to those they supposedly serve. Our policy elites maintain that they favor free markets while simultaneously battling against free markets on behalf of a world-changing ideology; they proclaim that they value traditional religion while fighting to undermine its most fundamental foundations; they argue that the world order must be maintained while shying away from the reality of international politics.

Klaus Schwab, the head of the World Economic Forum, supposedly a repository of free market thinking, declares that he and his friends will "serve not only self-interest, but we serve the community"; he then proceeds to leverage economic power on behalf of their preferred ideological outcomes. The result is both economic failure and ideological failure. Take, for example, the Biden administration's simultaneous demand that oil companies ramp up production and that we completely undermine oil and gas development over the next few years in order to fight global warming. Or, more immediately, take the German attempts to "green" their own economy while quietly outsourcing energy production to Russia—a policy so egregiously stupid that it has now resulted in Germany firing up coal plants again, now that Russia has cut off the oil supply.

On the social front, our institutional elite declare fealty to traditional institutions—church, family, localism—and then simultaneously insist that society remake itself in the most radical possible image. House Speaker Nancy Pelosi declares her fealty to Catholicism in the same sentence in which she militantly maintains her support for abortion-on-demand; President Joe Biden proclaims his own religiosity while simultaneously deploying his Department of Justice to target states that seek to prevent the confusion and mutilation of children based on nonsensical gender theory.

On the foreign policy front, our institutional leaders tell us that we must uphold the world order, then refuse to accept the consequences of that leadership. They rail against the evils of the Saudi Arabian regime while simultaneously intoning that the West must sign a deal with the Iranian terror regime, then end up visiting the Saudis to beg for more oil production. They declare their undying support for the Ukrainian government, then become wishy-washy about providing either the support necessary for its victory or an exit plan in case victory is unachievable. They look askance at the Chinese threat to Taiwan, then teach proper transgender pronoun use to members of the Navy.

In short, our institutional elites rely on the power of civilizational foundations that long predate them—free markets, religious values, military strength—to prop up failing ideas that undermine those foundations. The result is failure. The Left looks at the prevailing elite consensus and declares it dishonest: If the elites' principles mattered, they would fight free markets, religious values and military strength. The Right looks at the prevailing elite consensus and feels the same way: If the elites put aside their ideological commitments to leftism, they'd cement our civilizational foundations rather than keep eroding them.

Perhaps the center isn't holding because it *shouldn't* hold. That center has sought to enshrine its own power by taking from both the Left and the Right; it has no coherent ideology of its own. And that false center is now coming apart with centrifugal force, torn between those who believe in the fundamental institutions of the West and those who wish to see them supplanted.

Roe v. Wade Is History, but the Abortion Debate Reveals Rot at America's Center

June 29, 2022

This week, the Supreme Court of the United States issued a ruling overdue by some five decades, striking down Roe v. Wade (1973) and its constitutionally unsubstantiated "right to abortion." Writing for the 6-3 majority in Dobbs v. Jackson Women's Health Organization, Justice Samuel Alito stated, "The Constitution makes no reference to abortion, and no such right is implicitly protected by any constitutional provision … It is time to heed the Constitution and return the issue of abortion to the people's elected representatives."

Despite the media's wailing and gnashing of teeth, and despite Democrats' impotent roars of rage, the reality is that the Supreme Court decision was not extreme in any way. It did not reflect the most ardent desires of pro-lifers. It did not, for example, declare a right to life applicable to unborn children under the 14th Amendment's guarantee against the removal of "life, liberty or property, without due process of law." Nor did the decision follow the legally correct advice of Justice Clarence Thomas, who recommended trashing the Supreme Court doctrine of "substantive due process," a persistently and irritatingly vague rubric that generally acts as a pretext for courts to pursue their favored public policy objectives. The decision did not even suggest that the federal Congress had the power to regulate abortion in place of state laws.

No, the Dobbs ruling returns the status of the question of abortion to the status quo ante prior to Roe. Now states will decide how and when to regulate abortion. Some states, like Texas, will work to bar abortion except in cases in which the mother's life is in danger. Others, like New York, will cheer abortion up until the point of actual birth. No consensus policy is likely to emerge, because there is no consensus on the issue among Americans.

Yet Democrats and the media seem firmly convinced that the re-animation of abortion as a state law issue will somehow translate into 2022 electoral victory. There is little evidence to this effect: State laws generally reflect the opinions of those who live in those states, and the most ardent abortion defenders tend to reside in heavily blue areas where abortion will be freely available. It's hard to believe that Manhattan residents are going to show up to the polls en masse to vote on Alabama's abortion policy—and even if they did, it would make no difference in House or Senate elections in Ohio.

There is another problem for Democrats, too. That problem lies in the simple fact that if Americans *do* vote based on abortion, they don't do so purely based on preferred abortion policy. They do so based on the attitude of the parties toward abortion generally. And today, the party of abortion extremism is the Democratic Party, which long ago abandoned the logically unsound but emotionally appealing rubric of "safe, legal and rare," instead substituting the hideously monstrous "shout your abortion." The Democratic Party moved away from moral condemnation of abortion because Democrats now believe that human happiness is rooted in subjective self-definition, particularly with regard to sexual activity; that biology, particularly pregnancy and childbearing, is an active imposition on such a vision of human happiness; and that abortion is therefore a sacrament to be protected.

Few Americans outside of solid blue areas agree with these bizarre and ugly notions. So, while Democrats suggest that voters will resonate to their abortion messaging, fearful of abortion restrictions that might prohibit them from terminating their pregnancies, they miss a broader point: their vision of human happiness and the measures necessary to achieve it are not in line with that of most Americans. And that means that the culture war that the Left began is now turning against them, as it should.

Woke Academic Gobbledygook Makes You Rich and Famous

July 13, 2022

This week, a professor went viral during congressional testimony regarding the Supreme Court's Dobbs decision overruling Roe v. Wade. During her testimony, professor Khiara Bridges of Berkeley Law School refused to acknowledge any value at all in unborn children, instead stating, "I think that the person with the capacity for pregnancy has value and they should have the ability to control what happens." This prompted Sen. Josh Hawley, R-Mo., to ask, "You've referred to people with a capacity for pregnancy. Would that be women?" Bridges immediately responded, "Many cis women have the capacity for pregnancy. Many cis women do not have the capacity for pregnancy. There are also trans men who are capable of pregnancy as well as nonbinary people who are capable of pregnancy." Hawley asked incredulously, "Your view, the core of this right is about what?" To which Bridges shot back, "I want to recognize that your line of questioning is transphobic, and it opens up trans people to violence." She then blamed Hawley for the high suicidal ideation rate of those who identify as transgender, and lectured him, "We have a good time in my class. You should join."

Hawley was of course correct that only women can have babies; women who believe they are men are still women. And the notion that suicidal ideation rates among LGBT people are the result predominantly of societal bigotry is completely evidence-free; suicidal ideation rates among LGBT people remain massively higher than among cisgender heterosexual people in San Francisco just as they would in Alabama.

The question that should trouble us, then, isn't whether men have babies. They don't. The question is why our most prestigious academic institutions now churn out privileged pseudo-intellectuals who spout utter nonsense at the drop of the hat, and do it with self-assured sententiousness.

The answer lies in the incentive structure in higher education. Our higher education system is designed to benefit claims of victimhood rooted in intersectional identity politics. That is the only way to explain just why Bridges, one of the most educationally privileged members of American society, makes a career complaining about the systemic evils of the United States. It takes enormous gall and equal ignorance to claim that bigotry lies behind the reality of sexual dichotomy; it takes just as much gall and ignorance to claim that a country that has afforded you the opportunity to achieve a degree from Spelman College, a JD from Columbia Law School, a Ph.D. from Columbia in anthropology, and a career in classical ballet is somehow a country shot through with systemic racism.

And yet that is precisely what Bridges does for a living. Her study specializes in "race, class, reproductive rights, and the intersection of the three." Author of "Critical Race Theory: A Primer" and a self-described "critical race theorist," Bridges believes in the "rejection of legal conventions" and advocates in favor of the ideas that "racism is a normal feature of American society (and not a deviation from an otherwise fair and just status quo)" and that "traditional liberal understandings of the problem of racism and how racism will be defeated" ought to be rejected.

This, too, is nonsense. But it is nonsense cherished by the elite institutions that churn out supposed academics like Bridges. Our system of academia is irrevocably broken. Academia was originally perceived as a place of merit-based higher learning, a place in which the best and brightest formulated the most important policies. Academia was the West's intellectual oligarchy. But if the idea behind a merit-based academic elite used to rest in the actual merit of ideas and performance, that idea was left behind long ago. Now, the self-perpetuating academic elite is happy to maintain control by paying lip service to radicals like Bridges. All that matters, in true Foucault fashion, is power. That, presumably, is the reason why Bridges treats dissent as a form of violence—oligarchs usually do.

Intellectual oligarchs are no different. And the biggest casualty is truth.

The International Anti-Woke Backlash

September 28, 2022

This week, Italy prepared to welcome a new prime minister: 45-year-old Giorgia Meloni, leader of the right-wing Brothers of Italy party since 2014. Meloni is a populist conservative on issues ranging from marriage to immigration; she is a nationalist by philosophy and combatively passionate by temperament. A clip of a speech she gave at the World Congress of Families in 2019 has now gone viral with American conservatives; she explained, "Why is the family an enemy? Why is the family so frightening? There is a single answer to all these questions. Because it defines us. Because it is our identity. Because everything that defines us is now an enemy for those who would like us to no longer have an identity and to simply be perfect consumer slaves. And so they attack national identity, they attack religious identity, they attack gender identity, they attack family identity ... We will defend God, country and family."

This speech, according to much of the media, represented an indicator of incipient fascism in the land of Benito Mussolini. Never mind that former Italian prime minister Matteo Renzi scoffed at such a notion, calling the "risk of fascism ... absolutely fake news." The Intercept promptly called Meloni the "latest fascist womanhood icon." Ishaan Tharoor of The Washington Post railed that she's "set to be her country's most ultra-nationalist premier since fascist dictator Benito Mussolini."

Meloni is merely the latest recipient of such treatment internationally. In Sweden, the new government, supported by the right-wing Sweden Democrats, is already being touted as proto-fascist thanks to the origins of the SD. In Hungary, Prime Minister Viktor Orban has been treated as a knockoff of Vladimir Putin, despite the fact that he won his last election with a bare majority of 52.52% of the vote, increasing his vote share from 47.89% in 2018 and 44.87% in 2014. Polish Deputy Prime Minister Jaroslaw Kaczynski, leader of the Law and Justice Party, has been treated similarly; so have Brazilian President Jair Bolsonaro (currently trailing in the polls to socialistic former president Luiz Inacio Lula da Silva), and former and probable future Israeli Prime Minister Benjamin Netanyahu.

What, precisely, is the common thread linking these disparate politicians across a wide variety of countries? After all, none of these politicians are remotely like Vladimir Putin or Xi Jinping; none of them preside over authoritarian states. In fact, Left-wing politicians have engaged in far more intrusive antidemocratic measures over the past two years, from lockdowns to unilateral centralization of executive power.

The common thread is precisely the themes embraced by Meloni: national pride and rejection of Left-wing social values. The radical anti-traditionalism of the post-modernist Left, combined with the social apathy of centrists, has led to a serious international backlash. That backlash takes the form of a resurgent recognition that basic roles within societies must be protected, and that failure to do so is tantamount to national suicide.

And it is precisely that backlash that many in the media find so disquieting. To them, traditional roles are themselves fascist institutions; those who promote such roles suggest that human happiness can't be found in atomistic individualism, supplemented by collective social welfare schemes. And so true freedom requires that those like Meloni be fought.

Unfortunately for the Left, anti-traditionalism is the privilege of the frivolous—and after the failure of totalitarian COVID-19 policy, the collapse of green utopianism and the decay of societal solidarity, frivolity is no longer the order of the day. Which means that Meloni and those who agree with her are only the beginning.

Joe Biden, Dylan Mulvaney and the Collapse of the West

October 26, 2022

This week, President Joe Biden held an interview with a TikTok influencer named Dylan Mulvaney. Mulvaney is a man—a former Broadway star in "The Book of Mormon"—who less than a year ago decided that he was a woman. Ever since, he has made daily videos titled "Day X as a Girl." These videos range from the stereotypical (on Day 1, Mulvaney announces, wearing drag, that he has cried three times) to the bizarrely cringe-inducing (on Day 120, Mulvaney analyzes his nipple size, which has increased from "cute little nipples" to "pepperoni nipples"). And they have earned Mulvaney in excess of 8.4 million followers along with makeup deals from CeraVe, MAC, Neutrogena and Kate Spade.

Mulvaney's cosplaying as a woman also earned him an interview with the most powerful person on the planet. In that interview, Mulvaney asked Biden, "Do you think states should have the right to ban gender-affirming health care?" For those who are unaware of the medical euphemisms currently in practice, "gender-affirming health care" amounts to a slate of "treatments" including socially transitioning minor children, calling them by new names and pretending that they are members of the opposite sex; pumping minors full of cross-sex hormones and/or puberty blockers, with unknown long-term effects; progressing toward surgeries ranging from phalloplasties (fake penises attached to females) and mastectomies (removal of breasts) to vaginoplasties (removal of the penis and testes and creation of a fake vagina for males) to facial reconstruction surgeries.

Biden answered, "I don't think any state or anybody should have the right (to restrict that). As a moral question and as a legal question, I just think it's wrong."

As a moral question, the president of the United States told a man dressed as a woman and engaging in the most idiotic stereotypical behavior that it would be a deep wrong to deny life-altering treatments to confused minors.

How did we arrive at this point in American life? How did our country decline to the point that a geriatric dotard, representing the global hegemon, can declare it immoral to prevent genital mutilation of young people in the name of anti-scientific "gender theory"?

The answer is obvious: traditional values are losing.

They are losing because the best defense of tradition is *tradition itself.* And that defense has now been obliterated by a society dedicated to the proposition that tabula rasa quasi-intellectualism is a better policymaker than tradition. To state that we ought to abide by effective and useful age-old traditions is no longer seen as enough; we must come up with some sort of argument that fulfills the demands of Left-wing secular humanists. The burden of proof has been shifted from radicals who wish to tear down durable institutions—up to and including binary sex distinctions—to those who advocate for those institutions. Radicals need not explain how tearing down these institutions will create a better world. They need only criticize the existing arrangements as "intolerant" and "noninclusive."

This is a recipe for societal collapse. Experience and wisdom are our teachers; destroying those teachers in the name of tabula rasa pseudo-rationalism is disastrously foolish. As FA Hayek observed, "Experience comes to man in many more forms than are commonly recognized by the professional experimenter or the seeker after explicit knowledge … The appropriateness of our conduct is not necessarily dependent on our knowing why it is so."

That's not to say that there are no secular humanistic arguments against the insanity of gender theory—there are, and they are convincing, which is why even moderate liberals have turned against the most radical aspects of the Left-wing agenda. But the fact that social radicals have been able to push so far so fast is disturbing evidence that our entire traditional framework of thinking and acting has been undermined.

It must be restored. The burden of proof must be on those who wish to destroy, not on those who wish to maintain. This means that Americans must have confidence enough to say, "It's worked before, and it works still. I will not surrender it simply because you demand that I do so."

You Will Be Made to Celebrate

December 7, 2022

In March 2013, nearly a decade ago, in this space, I made a prediction.

"Within the next few months," I wrote, "Justice Anthony Kennedy will likely rule that same-sex marriage is mandated by the Constitution of the United States ... states will be forced to recognize same-sex marriages; same-sex marriage will enter the public-school lexicon; religious institutions will be forced to recognize same-sex marriages or lose their tax-exempt status. Religious Americans will be forced into violating their beliefs or facing legal consequences by the government."

Welp.

This month, the Congress is poised to pass a bill that would sanctify same-sex marriage; that same bill essentially argues that opposing same-sex marriage is akin to opposing interracial marriage, an act of bigotry. It provides no explicit bar on removal of tax-exempt status from religious institutions; it does not protect religious individuals in their daily lives.

Meanwhile, the Supreme Court considers whether to force a religious web designer to make a website celebrating a same-sex marriage. Several of the more conservative justices seek to draw a line between anti-discrimination law—laws on the state and federal level preventing "discrimination" on the basis of "sexual orientation"—and religious freedom. They do so by creating distinctions on the basis of expressive behavior (say, artistic expression in making a website) versus simple services provision (say, running a restaurant); they do so by distinguishing between services that require a message (say, baking a wedding cake) and serving gay couples without any message attached.

All of this legal hairsplitting is being done in an attempt to craft a form of the so-called Utah Compromise. That compromise put in place an anti-discrimination law with specific religious exemptions. But the Utah Compromise creates two additional problems: first, it stigmatizes belief in traditional marriage as a sort of vestige of religious bigotry we allow out of an outdated sympathy for the antiquated Bible-believers; second, it does not extend the rights of religious people outside of religious institutions. And, as it turns out, most religious people spend most of their time outside of religious institutions.

None of this would be necessary had we not undergone a complete transformation of the constitutional order over the past few decades. The Constitution of the United States provides zero power to the federal government to violate freedom of speech or association or religion. But, as Christopher Caldwell has pointed out in "The Age of Entitlement," the Civil Rights Act created a "rival Constitution" dedicated to violating those freedoms in the name of anti-discrimination. One can agree that racial bigotry is evil while still recognizing that the intrusion of the CRA into private behavior—not merely in ending state-sponsored discrimination, which was necessary and appropriate—amounts of a massive expansion of federal power in violation of the Constitution.

The legal obliteration of the distinction between governmental and private activity was only one prong of the new societal remolding. The second was the philosophical obliteration of the distinction between immutable characteristics and behavior. The case can easily be made morally that people ought not be victims of discrimination based on their immutable characteristics, like race; rejecting moral disapproval of particular behavior, however, means destroying the basis for any moral system. Yet that is what the law does when it likens race to sexual orientation philosophically.

These twin attacks on traditional American society—vitiation of the distinction between private and public, and elimination of the distinction between innate characteristics and behavior—are predicates to tyranny. The new secular system sets up government as a new god, determining right and wrong and cramming it down on every subject. You will be forced to celebrate the behaviors of others; you will be treated as a bigot if you do not. The Supreme Court may hold back the legal ramifications of the new tyranny for now, but anyone who relies on the court to do so forever will be sorely disappointed.

The Slippery Slope Never Ends

December 14, 2022

In 2006, then-Sen. Joe Biden ranted against the supposed irrelevance of a proposed constitutional amendment to define marriage in federal law as one man, one woman. "We already have a law, the Defense of Marriage Act," he said. "I've voted, and others have said, look, marriage is between a man and a woman and states must respect that. Nobody's violated that law, there's been no challenge to that law. Why do we need a constitutional amendment? Marriage is between a man and a woman."

Sixteen years later, President Joe Biden stood on the lawn of the White House and chortled that he had finally enshrined same-sex marriage into federal law. "Today's a good day," he said. "A day America takes a vital step toward equality, toward liberty and justice, not just for some, but for everyone."

A vital step. Not the final step. Not the culminating step. A vital step.

The language here is important because it is revealing. Biden and his allies have an agenda that goes far beyond the redefinition of marriage. The agenda is simple: use of government to obliterate traditional values and intermediary social institutions that embody them.

Biden made this clear in his speech, in which he lumped together opposition to same-sex marriage with "racism, antisemitism, homophobia, transphobia." This is patent nonsense, of course. But it does set the groundwork for the actual transgressive agenda: to liken traditional views about marriage to pure bigotry. And this will necessitate governmental action against those who believe in marriage. After all, we as a society don't tolerate racism on the basis of religious freedom. If Christian views about marriage are treated similarly, why *should* churches maintain their tax-exempt status while "discriminating" against same-sex weddings?

Biden went still further. In championing same-sex marriage, he said that Americans "need to challenge the hundreds of callous, cynical laws introduced in the states targeting transgender children, terrifying families and criminalizing doctors who get children the care they need." In other words, if you oppose the hormonal sterilization and surgical mutilation of minors as a pseudo-palliative for gender identity disorder, you are evil, and you must be stopped by force of federal law.

The natural outcome of this agenda will be precisely what Democrats pretend now to oppose: anti-religious discrimination, educational cramdowns, threats to traditional parenting. And make no mistake: they are pretending. They have no rationale for drawing lines to hem in their cultural imperialism. When asked by CBS News correspondent Steve Portnoy whether protections for religious practice were "codifying discrimination," White House press secretary Karine Jean-Pierre answered, "Is there more work to do? Absolutely. There's always more work to do."

In the early 1990s, Democrats denied that they wanted civil unions. They were lying. In the mid-2000s, Democrats denied that they wanted same-sex marriage. They were lying. Now Democrats say they don't want religious discrimination or educational indoctrination. They are lying. In the end, what transgressives want is simple: a national state that stands as the god of a new moral system, and atomized individuals without recourse to intermediary institutions of community or civil society.

And if the Republicans who voted for the Orwellian Respect for Marriage Act think that they have bought a respite from the predations of the Left by signing onto an erstwhile compromise, they will soon learn the error of their ways.

Young Americans Are Losing Their Minds. The Social Left Is to Blame.

February 15, 2023

This week, the Centers for Disease Control and Prevention released new data showing that our nation's young girls are in a state of absolute emotional and mental crisis. According to the CDC, 57% of high school girls said they were depressed in 2021, compared with 36% in 2011; 30% said they had considered suicide, compared with 19% in 2011. The numbers had also increased markedly for high school boys: 29% of high school boys reported depressive symptoms, up from 21% in 2011; 14% of high school boys had considered suicide, up from 13% a decade before.

Naturally, our nation's pseudoscientific experts blame societal intolerance and lack of sexual sensitivity. Never mind the fact that more kids than ever are declaring themselves members of nonexistent identity groups (Demisexual! Gender nonbinary!), mistakenly self-diagnosing with Tourette's syndrome or gender dysphoria, and claiming victimhood at the hands of a cruel society— a society that rewards and cheers all such claims. Never mind that we've now undergone a gender revolution in which we've declared biological sex itself passe, treated heterosexual norms as taboo and misogynistic and attempted to wipe away—along with actual sexual predation—much normal behavior in the name of #MeToo.

No, says the CDC, the problem—as always—is with society's demands. As The Wall Street Journal reports, the CDC recommends "teaching kids about sexual consent, managing emotions, and asking for what they need"; furthermore, "Schools should encourage gender and sexuality alliances, provide safe spaces and people for LGBTQ+ students to go to for support, and ensure enforcement of antiharassment policies."

Yes, the answer to five decades of social Leftism resulting in two generations unmoored from mental health is ... more social Leftism!

Or, alternatively, any society that attempts to destroy all rules, roles and intermediate institutions laden with traditional values will end up abandoning its children—all in the name of tolerance and diversity. We have robbed young men of a sense of meaning: we've told them that they need not be providers, protectors or defenders, and that even aspiring to do so makes them bigoted remnants of the past. Instead, young men are told that they ought to relegate themselves to the role of "male feminists," condemning their own "toxic masculinity" while shying away from the commitments that turn boys into men.

We have robbed young women of any sense of place, time or purpose: we've told them that they need not seek out a husband, aspire to bear and rear children or make preparations to build a home. Instead, we've told them that they can run from their own biology, declaring themselves boys rather than girls, delaying childbearing indefinitely, pursuing the things that are supposedly truly important: sexual license, more work hours, sipping wine at brunch with single friends.

We have done all of this because children do not lie at the top of our civilizational hierarchy: the interests of adults do. Increasingly, adults in the West see children as either a burden and thus avoid having them, or as validators of their own sense of subjective self-identity, requiring indoctrination into more liberal forms of social organization.

And now children are paying the price.

The social Left has been in control of virtually all levers of culture and policy for decades. Now they demand more control in order to alleviate the consequences of the chaos they have created. The answer, of course, is precisely the opposite: the reinvigoration of traditional sources of wisdom and values, the re-inculcation of morality and obligation. If our society does not quickly reverse field, the consequences for our young people will be utterly disastrous.

When a Trans Person Murders Christian Schoolchildren

March 29, 2023

The legacy media have a preset narrative machine when it comes to mass shootings. That narrative machine takes into account the identities of the shooter and the victims, and then churns out an explanation for the shooting. White shooter, black victims: systemic racism. Black shooter, white victims: alienation caused by systemic racism. Muslim shooter, gay victims: Christian homophobia.

On Monday, a self-identified 28-year-old trans man shot up a Christian school in Nashville, killing three children and three adults. The shooter left a manifesto, which police said reeked of "resentment." And so this week, we are learning what pops up in the narrative machine when the inputs are "trans man" and "Christian schoolchildren."

And here's what pops up: America is systemically cruel to trans people, who apparently cannot be blamed for losing control and targeting small children at Christian schools. A hate crime by a trans-identifying person against a religious group is immediately transmuted into a generalized societal crime against the mass shooter herself. Thus, NBC contributor Benjamin Ryan tweeted, "NBC has ID'd the Nashville school shooter ... Nashville is home to the Daily Wire, a hub of anti-trans activity by @MattWalshBlog, @BenShapiro and @MichaelJKnowles." Newsweek tweeted a story titled, "Tennessee Republicans' ban on drag shows criticized after mass shooting." ABC News correspondent Terry Moran stated that the shooter "identified herself as a transgender person. The State of Tennessee earlier this month passed and the governor signed a bill that banned transgender medical care for minors ..."

In the perverse world of Leftist victimology, this makes sense: If you are a member of a supposedly victimized group, you cannot be the victimizer; there must be another victimizer who has victimized you, turning you back into a victim.

But if we truly wish to prevent future acts of violence by unhinged lunatics, we ought to utilize a lens other than the lie of victimhood. Instead, we ought to consider the possibility that it is dangerous to promote the idea that mentally ill people ought to be celebrated as political groundbreakers by the legacy media for their symptoms, and simultaneously told that their suicidal ideations are caused by the intolerance of a broader society. According to a recent 2022 study, "Transgender and gender-diverse youth emerge as the group at the highest risk of support for violent radicalization." Teaching trans-identifying people that their suffering is caused by a cruelly religious and patriarchal world, explaining that these forces put their very lives in danger—that, indeed, they are victims of a potential "genocide"—creates an incredibly dangerous ideological predicate for violent action.

But the legacy media, by and large, support that narrative. To admit the obvious—that men cannot be women and vice versa; that believing you were born "in the wrong body" is a mental disorder, not a weapon to be used in tearing down an unjust society; that high rates of depression and suicidal ideation among those who identify as transgender is not caused predominantly by societal intolerance but by the disorder itself—undermines the new civil rights crusade the Left has built, directed against traditional roles and institutions.

And so the new narrative must be maintained. A woman who shot to death six people including three children in cold blood must be recast as a victim of society. We must respect "his" pronouns even as we report "his" murders. We must blame those who truly cause pain in the world: those who disagree with the thought leaders in our legacy media, who know better than all the common sense, biology and tradition in the world.

The Revolution at The Heart Of 'Pride'

June 7, 2023

June 1 marked the advent of Pride Month—the most important sacrament of the American secular religious calendar. During Pride Month, public schools across the nation teach small children the joys of alternative sexual practices and orientations; corporations plaster their stores in rainbow accoutrements of all sorts; and the federal government of the United States proclaims its fidelity to the LGBTQ+*&^% ideology.

The American public, for the most part, has historically taken Pride Month not for what it is but for what it sometimes purports to be: a call for tolerance of the marginalized. But that, of course, is not what Pride Month is or ever was. Pride Month is not a call for equality but a call for revolution. The Pride movement was always a call for a replacement of historic, tried and true cultural norms with new, untried and risky cultural norms.

Heteronormativity is one such tried and true norm: the correct belief that any durable society rests on the basis of male-female dyads producing children. Such a norm ought to be promoted. But Pride suggests the opposite: that heteronormativity is an authoritarian and discriminatory standard that places artificial limits on the full flowering of human sexuality. Explode the norm and maximize human happiness!

This, of course, was precisely the case made by the original exponents of the sexual revolution. Herbert Marcuse, author of "Eros and Civilization" (1955) called for a rewriting of all sexual norms in order to tear down the capitalist structure. He sought "a non-repressive civilization, based on a fundamentally different experience of being, a fundamentally different relation between man and nature, and fundamentally different existential relations." Such a civilization could only be birthed by treating "the body in its entirety (as) an object of cathexis, a thing to be enjoyed—an instrument of pleasure." Sex would be unmoored from marriage and parenthood; Marcuse argued, "the barriers against absolute gratification would become elements of human freedom ... This sensuous rationality contains its own moral laws."

By 1970, feminist Shulamith Firestone argued that sexual revolution would bring about "not just the elimination of male privilege but of the sex distinction itself: genital differences between human beings would no longer matter culturally." Happiness would now be found in a "reversion to an unobstructed pansexuality— Freud's 'polymorphous perversity'—would probably supersede hetero/homo/bi-sexuality."

We have now reached the dystopia sought by Marcuse and Firestone: a world in which all the elites in our society participate in the rewriting of durable societal norms in favor of unending sexual gratification. In order to maintain that dystopia, however, our societal elites require one more element: repression of the traditional norms. A fair fight might leave traditional Judeo-Christian norms in place; they've proved rather durable over time. Marcuse had a solution for just such a problem: repression. Promotion of the new morality would require quashing the old. "(L)iberation of the Damned of the Earth presupposes suppression not only of their old but also of their new masters," Marcuse wrote.

And so the culture war rages. Because, after all, old norms don't die easily. They must be killed in order to achieve "Pride" in the alternative. And that revolution requires the exercise of cultural, governmental and corporate power from sea to shining sea.

Do You Love America?

July 5, 2023

What, precisely, is it about America you love?

That's the question this July 4 as just 29% of Democrats say they're extremely proud of the country, accompanied by just 33% of Independents and 60% of Republicans. In fact, Democratic love of country has always fallen far behind that of Republicans, even during the Obama era, when it hit a temporary high of just over 50% (Republicans at the time said they were extremely proud of the country at a rate of approximately 70%).

Why is it that liberals in the United States are so much less proud of America than conservatives? These days, the answer typically given is America's inherent sinfulness; there is nothing in the American founding worth conserving. On Independence Day, Rep. Cori Bush, D-Mo., tweeted, "The Declaration of Independence was written by enslavers and didn't recognize Black people as human. Today is a great day to demand Reparations Now." Rep. Jamaal Bowman, D-N.Y., similarly tweeted, "This July 4th, we must remember that we stand on stolen land toiled by enslaved Africans and recommit ourselves to the fight for freedom, equality, & justice so that these ideals are accessible to everyone, not just a privileged few. We are not free until everyone is truly free."

America, to these types, is a platform for utopianism rather than a set of ideals worthy of emulation. The Declaration of Independence was a lie; the Constitution was merely a guise for power. And the quest for a perfect world must begin in tearing down such institutions with whatever means are at our disposal. The ends justify the means.

Thus, while Democrats fulminate over supposed threats to democracy, a federal judge this week ruled that the Biden administration violated the First Amendment in pressuring social media companies to restrict free speech regarding COVID-19 and the Hunter Biden laptop scandal, among others; the Supreme Court ruled that the Biden White House had violated its constitutional boundaries in waiving student loan debt. Biden's response: He pledged to utilize the executive branch to work around the Supreme Court's ruling.

Respect for the founding means respect for founding principles. Biden and his ilk have used a misinterpretation of one founding principle—"equality"—to vitiate the natural rights for which the founders originally fought. When the founders said that "all men are created equal," they meant specifically that human beings had been "endowed by their Creator with certain unalienable Rights, that among these are Life, Liberty and the pursuit of Happiness." They did *not* mean, as Biden suggests, that all human beings ought to be *made* equal in result, or that indeed, all human beings are equal in all capacities. Biden's idea is utopian nonsense; the founders' idea was grounded in millennia of evidence and Judeo-Christian tradition.

Patriots celebrate the founding for what it was: a breakthrough in the nature of human governance, a ringing statement in favor of liberty from the heavy hand of tyranny. Today, too many celebrate the founding only as a platform for future change—change that would annihilate the ideals of the founding along the road to a "higher good." This, presumably, is why Republicans are far more patriotic than Democrats even while saying that America is in the midst of a moral crisis; meanwhile, Democrats are far less patriotic while suggesting pride in America's current moral state. Conservatives are disappointed with man's sinfulness, but proud of the founders' ideals; many liberals are disappointed with the founders' ideals, and proud of man's sinfulness.

How Burning Man Became Uncool

September 6, 2023

This week, the Burning Man festival—a convocation of large groups of men and women seeking sex, drugs, rock 'n' roll and other forms of hedonistic bliss—was flooded. It seems that a half-inch of rain swamped the event, which takes place in the Black Rock Desert in Nevada, turning the dust to deep and sticky mud. The images of barely clad neo-hippies struggling to walk through the muck spread like wildfire across the internet; even the White House was forced to acknowledge that it was monitoring the situation.

For a huge swath of Americans, all of this was simply amusing. But the rise and mainstreaming of Burning Man is a far more interesting story than its pathetic possible demise. Burning Man was founded in 1986, when some hippie types gathered at the beach in San Francisco to burn a nine-foot-tall wooden man. Over time, the bonfire became larger and larger, until eventually it moved to Nevada, where it has been located ever since. Each year, 100,000 people head out to the middle of the desert to participate in events ranging from impromptu art exhibits to orgies and mass drug use.

The fundamental principles of Burning Man are spelled out in co-founder Larry Harvey's 10 Principles, written in 2004. These principles construct a paganistic morality built around a bevy of mutually exclusive notions. For example, Burning Man is about "radical inclusion … No prerequisites exist for participation in our community." But Burning Man is also "devoted to acts of gift giving." Unfortunately, without some form of mutuality, giving alone cannot form the basis of a functioning society, even temporarily. All of which means that Burning Man features social pressure to ostracize free-riders—a tragic violation of the radical inclusion principle.

Burning Man values "radical self-expression," which cannot be defined by anyone other "than the individual or a collaborating group." But such radical self-expression quickly comes into conflict with Burning Man's call for "civic responsibility," which surely encroaches on the unlimited right to self-expression. Burning Man also values "immediacy," which it calls "the most important touchstone of value in our culture." But Burning Man also calls for the community to "clean up after ourselves," which runs directly counter to the premise of immediacy.

All of this would be sheer countercultural nonsense, except for one perverse fact: The counterculture has now become the culture. This accounts for the fact that Burning Man now seems tired and played out, less transgressive than wearied. The age of Burning Man attendees has increased over the past decade (average age in 2013 was 32, compared to 37 just nine years later); so has the average income (in 2006, 14% of Burners listed their personal income at above $100,000, compared to 27.4% by 2016). Influencers now show up at Burning Man to sell Popeye's Spicy Chicken; Elon Musk, Paris Hilton and Mark Zuckerberg have shown up.

And herein lies the problem for the broader American culture. Our elite class used to be inculcated in the same set of baseline values as "normal" Americans: John D. Rockefeller was a regular churchgoer; so was Cornelius Vanderbilt. Today, our elites participate in drug-fueled binges in the desert—or at least wish to appear as though they do. Throughout the 1930s, even the poorest Americans aspired to dress well, wearing suits even on the breadlines. Today, even the richest Americans dress as though they shop at Salvation Army.

When elites promulgate countercultural garbage that eats at the roots of fundamental societal institutions, societal bonds dissolve. Ironically, that dissolution occurs first at the lowest rungs of the income ladder: As Charles Murray points out, "The belief that being a good American involved behaving in certain kinds of ways, and that the nation itself relied upon a certain kind of people in order to succeed, had begun to fade and has not revived." In fact, those who live out lives of good decision-making are, all too often, embarrassed of their good choices. To promote those choices might seem "judgmental."

That is the real tragedy of Burning Man: its mainstreaming.

Every society has its oddball behaviors. Only sick societies incentivize their imitation.

The Apple Vision Pro Future

February 7, 2024

This week, I tried out the Apple Vision Pro.

That's the device you've been seeing on the news: the bulky, unwieldy headgear; the bizarre images of people attempting to manipulate the air in front of them; even some people driving while looking like Geordi La Forge from "Star Trek."

It's extraordinary.

As a piece of technology, I've never seen anything like it. It takes the apps on your phone and places them in the world around you: you can pin them in various rooms in your home. This essentially makes television extraneous; it allows you to post lists of groceries on your refrigerator; it allows you to speak with people in real-time while navigating the real world. The graphics are in the early stages, but they're just as mind-boggling: one app called Encounter Dinosaurs introduces you into a prehistoric landscape, complete with dinosaurs. Remember how terrible movie 3D is? This is *nothing* like that. It's totally immersive, and reacts to you.

So, what does this mean?

On a raw level, it means that entertainment like movies and gaming will be leagues better than anything now available. You'll be fighting with a lightsaber like Luke Skywalker in "Star Wars"; you'll be surfing waves along with Kelly Slater. You'll also be in landscapes far from your office or cubicle—you can already seat yourself in the midst of a nature landscape near Mount Hood, complete with soundscapes and full 360-degree view.

But as the technology progresses, it means something far more dangerous: the complete transformation of human relations.

Why? Because right now, everyone knows that you're engaging in a mixed reality; after all, you look like an idiot wearing around scuba gear in broad daylight. But presumably, the technology will get smaller and less obtrusive. It's not hard to foresee a future when people will have all the same capabilities and more, but projected into contact-lens type technologies.

And when that happens, everything changes.

Imagine walking around, being able to access answers to any question by referring to ChatGPT—without anyone knowing you're doing so. Every conversation becomes a supplemented conversation. Every job interview becomes a test of AI rather than a test of the human being. Every date becomes a date between two AI prompts. Or imagine a shared reality in which everyone wearing the technology sees the filters projected by others—so that normal human appearance disappears, corrected by the technology toward the unobtainable ideal. Imagine an even more dystopian world in which Apple or another major corporation controls what you see and hear by barring certain content or mandating certain language.

The world of supplemented reality can open new vistas. But it can also become jet fuel for human frailty and sin, the same way smartphones have been. Imagine children growing up with such technology, removed from the normal consequences of life, their thinking atrophied by AI superpower, never having experienced the difficulty and beauty of normal human relationships.

We are opening a can of worms here. And that can of worms can't be closed. All of which means that even as our society throws away classical virtue, nothing is more necessary than its rapid reinstitution. If we advance technology and give people new capacities while ignoring the natural limitations of human beings, we are likely to meet with the ugly consequences of unknown unknowns.

Racing to Declare Racism

Racial Reparations Solve Nothing

January 18, 2023

This week, the San Francisco African American Reparations Advisory Committee released a report calling on the city to pay every black resident $5 million and absolve all of their outstanding personal debt. Their rationale was broad—as it had to be, since California was founded as a free state: "While neither San Francisco, nor California, formally adopted the institution of chattel slavery, the tenets of segregation, white supremacy and systematic repression and exclusion of Black people were codified through legal and extralegal actions, social codes, and judicial enforcement."

This rationale serves as the same sort of catchall term as "equity," widely beloved by the political Left. It conflates specific harms from deliberate policies—which deserve redress—with vague societal ills that indirectly and unverifiably impact the specific life paths of individuals. Thus, every inequality between blacks and whites, for example, becomes an instance of societal failure, to be cured with social engineering.

This is bad ethics, and it is bad social science. It's bad ethics because the innocent should not be forced to pay people against whom they have not sinned, and because the connection between continued suffering and past discrimination must be measured and clarified rather than merely assumed. It's bad social science because it ignores the role of individual decision-making in persistent intergenerational inequality, despite the massive intervention of state, local and federal government.

Simply put, the preferred solution of San Francisco's reparations committee—simply cutting checks—has been a dramatic failure in the United States. In 1965, speaking at Howard University, President Lyndon Baines Johnson explained that he wanted to pursue a program of widespread redistributionism in order to right the racial wrongs of the past: "You do not take a person who, for years, has been hobbled by chains and liberate him, bring him up to the starting line of a race and then say, 'you are free to compete with all the others,' and still justly believe that you have been completely fair."

To that end, the federal government has spent in excess of $25 trillion on redistribution programs in the United States. The result has been exceedingly poor: While the income gap ratio between the poorest quintile of Americans and the wealthiest quintile of Americans post-transfer payments and taxes is just 4-to-1, the wealth gap between black and white Americans has skyrocketed from approximately $50,000 pre-1960 to well over $130,000 in 2016. Why? Because it turns out that public policy designed to alleviate inequality can also alleviate the consequences of bad decision-making. If we assume that all inequality is inequity, then solving inequality should alleviate inequity—but if it turns out that a great deal of inequality is the result of bad decision-making, then inequality cannot be solved by simply helicoptering money to those at the bottom end of the economic ladder.

And yet the Left continues to do precisely that. Then they wonder why intergenerational wealth creation has not narrowed the racial gap. Perhaps it has something to do with the fact that 70% of black children are born to unwed mothers; nearly 8 out of 100 black males drop out of school; black college students tend to major in subjects that result in worse job prospects (just 12% of black students get a bachelor's degree in STEM, compared with 33% of Asian students and 18% of white students, for example); one-third of the American prison population is black.

It is possible to blame all of this on systemic evil, but any fixes will have to come at the level of individuals making good and responsible decisions. Cutting checks won't fix this. But such a policy recommendation makes for excellent demagoguery: It allows those who promote foolish and failed ideas to revel in their own supposed altruism, all while helping no one.

When Black Police Officers Kill a Black Man, That's White Supremacy

February 1, 2023

This week, tape emerged from Memphis, Tennessee of five black police officers engaging in the beating of Tyre Nichols, a 29-year-old black man. Nichols was pulled over for reckless driving according to the officers; they ordered him to get on the ground and to give them his hands; he did not comply and instead began to run. When the officers caught up with him, they pummeled him, complete with strikes to the head while his hands were being held behind his back. Nichols died in the hospital.

The five officers involved were charged with second-degree murder, kidnapping, official misconduct and official oppression. All were fired from the police department.

The national media coverage was swift—and confused. For some in the media, the narrative was clear: the police are generally brutal, and thus must be dramatically curbed. "The issue here, as plenty of people have pointed out, is not black versus white, it's blue versus the rest of us," said MSNBC's Mehdi Hasan. "You can't reform this stuff with body cameras or diversifying the police, as we just saw in Memphis." Instead, Hasan suggested, abolition of the police might be a possible solution.

This solution, of course, is no solution at all: Memphis has one of the highest crime rates in the United States. According to Neighborhood Scout, the chances of becoming a victim of violent or property crime in the city are one in 12. And we know with statistical near-certainty that high-profile cases of police misconduct generally result in police stand-downs—which in turn result in more crime. As professors Tanaya Devi and Roland Freyer found in 2020, "all investigations that were preceded by 'viral' incidents of deadly force have led to a large and statistically significant increase in homicides and total crime."

A second media narrative quickly emerged from the Nichols killing: despite the fact that all involved were black, that the Memphis Police Department is majority black, that the chief of police is black—the killing was a result of "white supremacy." The Washington Post headlined, "Black Memphis police spark dialogue on systemic racism in the US." Van Jones opined at CNN.com, "The police who killed Tyre Nichols were Black. But they might still have been driven by racism." Kimberle Crenshaw, founder of intersectionality, explained, "One cannot imagine this happening in a well-heeled white community. That is a racial problem that the law has consistently said is a non-problem."

This narrative, like the first, is designed to avoid solutions. If all policing is the result of structures of white supremacy, the only answer is to abolish policing. If each individual instance of police brutality, no matter the race of the officers, is an example of racism, then the only way to alleviate police brutality is by completely restructuring American society—which is just what those like Crenshaw propose. The result won't be a safer America, but a much less safe and more fractious one.

In reality, instances of police brutality cross races. Whether it's Daniel Shaver being shot to death in a hotel while attempting to comply with police demands in 2016 or whether it's two Arkansas Sheriff's Deputies beating Randal Worcester in August 2022, white victims of police brutality aren't hard to find. Some police brutality can undoubtedly be curbed by better recruitment and training. But if we wish to actually lower the number of encounters between a given population and the police, thus reducing the number of possible violent interactions, the most obvious method would be to reduce criminal activity—which requires *more* policing and *more* law-abiding behavior.

None of this should be controversial. But solutions aren't what advocates of police abolition or critical race theory are looking for. They're looking for revolution. And all revolutions have casualties.

The Left's Favorite Lie: Widespread White-On-Black Violence

April 19, 2023

This week, a 16-year-old boy named Ralph Yarl—black—accidentally rang the doorbell of an 84-year-old white man, Andrew Lester. According to reports, Lester then shot Yarl twice through the door, wounding him in the head and the arm. According to Clay County prosecutor Zachary Thompson, "I can tell you there was a racial component."

This fact pattern immediately sent the salivary glands of the media and the Biden administration into overdrive. Drooling with excitement, the media headlined the Yarl shooting for days; President Joe Biden himself immediately invited Yarl, who survived, to the White House.

The reason for the journalistic and political feeding frenzy is clear: For the political Left, the narrative of white supremacy must be maintained. What's more, shocking examples of that narrative must be found. Yarl's shooting fit the bill. Americans are supposed to believe, as Yarl's attorney put it, that "blackness is under attack."

This is a lie. Not only is it a lie, it is a blatantly idiotic and devastatingly counterproductive lie. That lie provides the impetus toward undercutting police presence in high-crime areas; it provides the basis for racially discriminatory governmental policies; it provides the foundation for the argument that all disparities between the races are the result of white discrimination.

The truth is far more troubling: In America, while most violent crime is intra-racial (white on white or black on black, for example), in cases in which blacks and whites have violent interaction, blacks are overwhelmingly the perpetrators, not the victims.

In 2019, for example, 3,299 white Americans were murdered;

566, or 17%, were killed by black perpetrators. That same year, 2,906 black Americans were murdered; 246, or 8%, were killed by white perpetrators. Adjusted for population size—there are far more whites in America (235 million) than blacks (47 million)—this means that approximately one out of every million white Americans killed a black person in 2019, while 12 out of every million black Americans killed a white person. Such numbers are reflective of a norm: every year from 2001 on, the number of black-on-white killings has approximately doubled the number of white-on-black killings. When it comes to violent crime generally, the same sad truth applies. In 2019, there were 562,550 reported violent black/white incidents. 472,570 were black on white—84%.

The media routinely ignore these facts, since they don't fit the narrative. In fact, the media have a general tendency not to even mention the race of perpetrators of crimes if those perpetrators are black. The people harmed most by this narrative failure are not white Americans, but black Americans, who are predominantly the victims of black crime. According to the Department of Justice, "In 2018, based on data from the FBI's Uniform Crime Reporting (UCR) Program, black people were overrepresented among persons arrested for nonfatal violent crimes (33%) and for serious nonfatal violent crimes (36%) relative to their representation in the U.S. population (13%)." The vast majority of victims were black.

Understanding the facts about interracial crime presents different solutions than the lies we hear about the prevalence of white-on-black violence. Those solutions include encouraging fatherhood in the home. Only 37% of black children are living in a home with their biological parents; 72% of black fathers aren't married to the mother of their children; and only 4.2% of black children grow up in areas with a poverty rate below 10% and over half of black fathers present in the community.

But such discussions never take place if we focus on a lie: the lie that black victims are disproportionately the victim of white evils. Those who promulgate that lie victimize all Americans, black and white.

When You Don't Police Crime, Civilians Will

May 4, 2023

This week, the media found its latest iteration of its favorite narrative: white man harms black man. That iteration featured a 24-year-old white Marine from Queens attempting to suppress a 30-year-old homeless, psychotic black man, Jordan Neely, via use of a suppression hold. Neely was apparently threatening people on the subway when the Marine took him down from behind, keeping him in the suppression hold for 15 minutes; Neely died shortly thereafter.

The extraordinarily inflammatory and insipid Rep. Alexandria Ocasio-Cortez, D-N.Y., immediately rushed to Twitter in order to gin up outrage: "Jordan Neely was murdered. But bc Jordan was houseless and crying for food in a time when the city is raising rents and stripping services to militarize itself while many in power demonize the poor, the murderer gets protected w/ passive headlines + no charges. It's disgusting." Meanwhile, Manhattan Borough President Mark Levine tweeted, "I saw Jordan Neely perform his Michael Jackson routine many times on the A train. He always made people smile. Our broken mental health system failed him. He deserved help, not to die in a chokehold on the floor of the subway."

So, who was Neely? A career criminal. He wasn't just shouting threats at passengers—he had been arrested more than 40 times in the past. Those arrests ranged from drugs to disorderly conduct to fare beating. When he died, he carried an outstanding warrant for assaulting a 67-year-old woman. A bevy of people apparently report that he had attempted to shove people onto subway tracks more than once.

Why was Neely out on the streets? It was clear to everyone that he was a mentally ill psychotic man with a serious drug record, a rap sheet longer than the phone book and an alleged history of violent incidents. The answer is that the city of New York has decided no longer to prosecute crime. To do so might raise the unpalatable spectacle of racial disparity in crime statistics—and it is apparently more important to preserve egalitarianism in arrest statistics than to take active threats off the streets.

The consequences of such idiocy are dire, for both the general public and for people like Jordan Neely. How long can the authorities in New York expect everyday citizens to experience hostile and violent encounters before taking action? Commentator Toure tweeted, "It is normal to see loud, disturbing mental breakdowns on the NYC subway. I'm not defending that; I'm saying it's a regular occurrence. What's not normal is to murder people having loud, disturbing mental breakdowns." But short of prophecy, how can those watching such a breakdown, complete with threats against others, know who is harmless and who isn't? Normally such questions are outsourced to law enforcement. When law enforcement is prevented from doing its job, crime rises—and citizens are forced to engage in acts of self-defense.

All of this would be perfectly obvious were Jordan Neely white and the Marine black in this case; then, the media and political class would declare the Marine a hero for protecting others on the subway car. But the narrative must be preserved—the lie that crime by minority members must be ignored for the greater good of society, lest response to such crime facilitate systemic racism. Often, it's innocent victims who pay the price. In the case of Jordan Neely, it was the criminal himself, who never would have died were the system rational enough to have policed him decently years ago.

The Fight Against Faith

The Death of Eternal Truths and the New Paganism

January 4, 2023

Last week, Pope Benedict XVI died at the age of 95, nearly a decade after stepping down as head of the Catholic Church. His life was marked by adherence to a belief in an eternal truth above all. As he stated in a 2008 meeting with Catholic educators at the Catholic University of America, "Truth means more than knowledge: knowing the truth leads us to discover the good … (W)e observe, with distress, the notion of freedom being distorted. Freedom is not an opting out. It is an opting in—a participation in Being itself. Hence authentic freedom can never be attained by turning away from God."

There is a truth; that truth must be pursued; the only substitute for truth is falsehood. Human beings have sussed out eternal truths over the course of millennia, and to discard those truths in favor of subjectivism is crippling. Those eternal truths are rooted in the belief that God made us in His image; that He granted us roles and responsibilities; and that true freedom lies in making choices within the boundaries of those roles and responsibilities.

What happens when we discard those truths?

Disaster strikes.

First, we lose belief in something Higher; then we lose belief in ourselves.

We are seeing the consequences of this two-step process before us in real time.

In a recent interview with The Wall Street Journal, social psychologist Jonathan Haidt spelled out what happens when we turn our gaze inward rather than outward. Generation Z, he said, has been sucked into a vortex of narcissism and jealousy and isolation.

According to Haidt, there has "never been a generation this depressed, anxious and fragile." For girls, particularly, replacement of roles with constant self-assessment has been a pathway to hell: "You post your perfect life, and then you flip through the photos of other girls who have a more perfect life, and you feel depressed." The new cultural ideology "valorizes victimhood ... You're not going to take chances, you're going to ask for accommodations, you're going to play it safe, you're not going to swing for the fences, you're not going to start your own company."

Civilizationally, the loss of inherited wisdom and traditional values has resulted in new, ersatz gods to worship. The most obvious god is the pantheistic god of nature, revenging itself on us for our capitalist excesses. Why else would "60 Minutes" feature widely discredited false green Paul R. Ehrlich, author of "The Population Bomb"? Ehrlich famously stated in 1968 that billions would die of starvation in the 1970s and 1980s; now, half a century later, he explains, "Humanity is not sustainable. To maintain our lifestyle (yours and mine, basically) for the entire planet, you'd need five more Earths. Not clear where they're gonna come from."

Never mind that Ehrlich is wrong. The real question is why he is still respected. The answer, of course, is that every religion requires its prophets, and the neopaganism of environmental catastrophism is no exception.

As the West loses its links with traditional wisdom, it breaks loose of its philosophical moorings. The consequences will be dire unless those moorings are reinforced. And they can only be reinforced by those who have the courage to defend eternal truths—not merely hide behind the tolerance of pluralism, a repository for the cowardice of conservatives who correctly stand with free speech but incorrectly think that stance sufficient to win the day.

In the end, either the truth will win out, or it will be destroyed. As Pope Benedict XVI told the Bishops of the United States in 2012, "The Church in the United States is called, in season and out of season, to proclaim a Gospel which not only proposes unchanging moral truths but proposes them precisely as the key to human happiness and social prospering." Defenders of traditional values of all stripes are called to the same quest.

Palestinian Arab Terrorism and The West's Moral Apathy

April 12, 2023

This week, Jews all over the world marked Passover, the celebration of the Jewish exodus from Egypt. As we congregated around seder tables to read from the "Haggadah"—the compendium of texts telling the story of the exodus—we said the following words: "And this (God's blessings and the Torah) is what kept our fathers and what keeps us. For not only one arose and attempted to destroy us, but in each generation, they stand to destroy us, and God saves us from their hands."

The Dee family, a family of seven originally from Great Britain but now from Efrat, Israel—the so-called West Bank, the heart of Biblical Israel—undoubtedly said the same words. Then, on Friday, Rina Dee (15), Maia Dee (20) and their mother Lucy (48) went on a drive through the Jordan Valley on the way to Tiberias, just miles from where Joshua would have brought the Jews across the Jordan River. There, they were attacked and shot to death by a Palestinian Arab terrorist who riddled their car with 20 bullets.

Hamas, the governing Palestinian party in the Gaza Strip and a powerful force in Palestinian Arab areas of Judea and Samaria, celebrated the murders. "We congratulate the Jordan Valley operation and warn the occupation against continuing its aggression against our Palestinian people and the blessed Al-Aqsa Mosque," they said. Meanwhile, husband and father Rabbi Leo Dee gave a eulogy for half of his family: "Let the Israeli flag today send out a message to humanity which is: We will never accept terror as legitimate. We will never blame the murder on the victims. There is no such thing as moral equivalence between terrorist and victim."

Sadly, the media played the moral equivalence game, treating the murder of two sisters and their mother as yet another round in the supposed "cycle of violence" between Israelis and Palestinian Arabs. Of course, in that "cycle of violence," Palestinian Arab terrorists target innocent civilians and then hand out candies when they achieve their evil goals, while the Israeli Defense Forces seek to root out and destroy terrorists. But to the media, it's all the same. "Daughters of British rabbi die in West Bank drive by shooting," touted The Sunday Times (U.K.), leaving no explanation for who had committed the shooting or why. "Two British sisters killed and mother injured in West Bank shooting," tut-tutted The Guardian; "2 killed in West Bank after Israel strikes Lebanon, Gaza," the Associated Press lied by omission.

The Biden administration has been little better. In recent weeks, as terrorism metastasized, the Biden administration urged Israel to "de-escalate," as though any state could ignore its moral duty to defend its citizens from routine acts of terrorism. Instead, the Biden administration summoned Michael Herzog, Israel's U.S. ambassador, to stress "the importance of all parties refraining from actions or rhetoric that could further inflame tensions leading into the Ramadan, Passover and Easter holidays."

This vile moral equivalence motivates terrorists to murder civilians and step up other violence. After all, there's no downside. When the media treat legitimate self-defense as terrorism and terrorism as legitimate self-defense, terrorists thrive. And they are thriving today, raising the specter of violence all across Israel: 18 civilians have been slaughtered by terrorists in Israel since Jan. 27. As terror increases, the necessity for larger-scale intervention grows, too. Then, the same media and Left-wing governments will decry the "cycle of violence" again, fostering yet more terrorism.

In every generation, the story is the same: In each generation, there are those who seek to destroy the Jews, and in every generation, through the grace of God, they fail. But that doesn't relieve those who retain any measure of decency from standing up against evil terrorists. The alternative is apathetic complicity—and that apathetic complicity costs lives.

Notes From Auschwitz

January 24, 2024

This week, I visited Auschwitz.

I had never before visited any of the death camps. The experience is absolutely chilling. Auschwitz, of course, was a complex of camps, the three largest of which were Auschwitz I, the camp most famous for the terrifyingly Orwellian German slogan welded onto its entrance, "ARBEIT MACHT FREI"; Auschwitz II, also known as Birkenau, the massive death factory at which the Germans operated four large gas chambers, each of which could be used to murder 2,000 people at a time; and Auschwitz III, a large labor camp. Visiting in January, with the ice covering the ground, is a reminder of the cruelties that are possible when human beings commit to the perverse disease of Jew-hatred.

Auschwitz was liberated some 79 years ago this month. But that perverse disease is alive and well. As survivor Marian Turski says, "Auschwitz did not fall suddenly from the skies, it was all tiny steps approaching until what happened here behind me did happen."

That gradualism masked the greatest evil in world history. As we descended into Krakow for the visit, I read the diaries of Victor Klemperer, a secular, intermarried Jew who had converted to Protestantism and who lived in Dresden during the period of Hitler's rule. Klemperer details the slow but steady changes that turned Jews into outcasts, no matter their ideology or even religious practice. Klemperer, for his part, considered himself a good German and the Nazis the outliers; even in 1942, Klemperer wrote, "I am fighting the most difficult of battles for my German-ness now. I must hold on to it: I am German, the others are un-German."

His protestations meant nothing.

Why?

Because Jew-hatred is and was a conspiracy theory rooted in the supposed power of the Jew. And there is nothing new about that theory; it is seductive and easy and ancient. In Egypt, Pharaoh spoke thus: "Look, the children of Israel are too numerous and large for us. Let us deal shrewdly with them, so that they may not increase." In Persia, Haman told Ahasuerus, "There is a certain people, scattered and dispersed among the other peoples in all the provinces of your realm, whose laws are different from those of any other people and who do not obey the king's laws." In Poland, Bogdan Chmielnicki told the Poles that they had been sold by the Polish nobility "into the hands of the accursed Jews." In Russia, the bestselling "Protocols of the Elders of Zion" alleged a Jewish conspiracy to exploit and control the gentile world. In Germany, Hitler wrote that the Jews sought to make the gentile world "ripe for the slave's lot of permanent subjugation." Today, across the Muslim world, the toxic proposition that the Jews control the world is a popular notion and provides justification for murderous terrorist attacks on Jewish civilians: according to a recent poll from the Arab Center for Research and Policy Studies, only 5% of all Middle Eastern and North African Arabs condemned Oct. 7 as an "illegitimate operation."

Across time and place, such ideas sprang from religion, from ethnic polarization, from nationalistic excess. Today, at least in the West, such ideas spring from an ideology that suggests a hierarchy of oppression that dominates Western societies, in which disproportionately successful groups are victimizers and disproportionately unsuccessful groups the victimized. It is no coincidence that LGBTQ+ and BLM activists, who propagate that victim/victimizer narrative, side with the genocidal Jew-hating terror group Hamas. According to a recent Harvard/Harris poll, some 67% of people aged 18-24 in the United States say that the Jews "as a class are oppressors and should be treated as oppressors."

Visiting Auschwitz, one can see the apex results of such perverse ideas. Another Holocaust may not be right around the corner; geopolitical conditions are not what they were in 1940, and no serious power has the means and capacity to accomplish anything like the Holocaust today (though Iran armed with a nuclear bomb would be a different story). But certainly the slogan "Never Again" cannot be used by those who currently hand-wave the atrocities of

Oct. 7 in the name of fighting supposed "Jewish power." The only way to stop Jew-hatred is to stop conspiratorial thinking—particularly the conspiratorial thinking of those in the West who despise meritocracy itself and instead see the mirage of the "powerful Jew" hiding behind every problem.

The Cut Flowers Civilization

April 3, 2024

This week, famed atheist Richard Dawkins explained that he was a "cultural Christian." Praising his civilization, Dawkins stated, "I do think that we are culturally a Christian country. I call myself a cultural Christian. I'm not a believer. But there is a distinction between being a believing Christian and being a cultural Christian. And so you know I love hymns and Christmas carols, and I sort of feel at home in the Christian ethos. I feel that we are a Christian country in that sense." Dawkins went on to praise Christianity as a "fundamentally decent religion in a way that I think Islam is not."

Dawkins' case for Christianity—a case made on the basis of utility—is nothing new. It was made long ago by acidic critic of the church Voltaire, who famously averred, "If God did not exist, it would be necessary to invent him." But the problem with the utilitarian case for religious belief is that it doesn't *animate religious believers.(*END ITAL) It is simply impossible to build a civilization on the basis of Judeo-Christian foundations while making the active case as to why those foundations ought to be dissolved.

In fact, Western civilization has doomed itself so long as it fails to reconnect to its religious roots. Philosopher Will Herberg wrote, "The moral principles of Western civilization are, in fact, all derived from the tradition rooted in Scripture and have vital meaning only in the context of that tradition. … Cut flowers retain their original beauty and fragrance, but only so long as they retain the vitality that they have drawn from their now severed roots; after that is exhausted, they wither and die. So with freedom, brotherhood, justice and personal dignity—the values that form the moral foundation of our civilization. Without the life-giving power of the faith out of which they have sprung, they possess neither meaning nor vitality."

We are a cut flowers civilization.

And eventually, cut flowers die.

That has never been more obvious than this week, when the Biden administration decided to honor the newly invented Transgender Day of Visibility on Easter Sunday. Gender ideology is a symptom of our society's reversion to gnostic paganism, in which unseen, chaotic forces buffet us about, and in which nature is directly opposed to the freedom of our disembodied essences. It is no wonder that gender ideology is opposed by every mainstream traditional religion.

Yet claiming that this magical holiday could not be moved, the White House issued a variety of statements in celebration of radical gender ideology, including the deeply insulting statement from the president of the United States citing the book of Genesis to the effect that transgender people are "made in the image of God"—ignoring the last half of the Biblical verse, which reads, "male and female he made them." What better time than Easter, the holiest day in the Christian calendar, to pay homage to an entirely new religion?

Richard Dawkins is obviously correct that a civilization rooted in church is better than a civilization rooted in an alternative set of values. But in reality, the churches cannot be empty; they must be full. The cathedrals that mean Britain to Dawkins must ring with the sounds of hymns in order to maintain their holiness and their importance; otherwise, they are merely beautiful examples of old architecture, remnants of a dead civilization preserved in stone.

But our civilization must live. And that means more than cultural Christianity. It means reengaging with the source of our values—the Scriptures that educated our fathers and grandfathers.

About the Author

Ben Shapiro was born in 1984. He entered the University of California Los Angeles at the age of 16 and graduated summa cum laude and Phi Beta Kappa in June 2004 with a Bachelor of Arts degree in Political Science. He graduated Harvard Law School cum laude in June 2007.

Shapiro was hired by Creators Syndicate at age 17 to become the youngest nationally syndicated columnist in the United States. His columns are printed in major newspapers and websites including The Riverside Press-Enterprise and the Conservative Chronicle, Townhall.com, ABCNews.com, WorldNetDaily.com, Human Events, FrontPageMag.com, and FamilySecurityMatters.com. His columns have appeared in The Christian Science Monitor, Chicago Sun-Times, Orlando Sentinel, The Honolulu Advertiser, The Arizona Republic, Claremont Review of Books, and RealClearPolitics.com. He has been the subject of articles by The Wall Street Journal, The New York Times, The Associated Press, The Christian Science Monitor and many more publications.

Shapiro is the author of best-sellers "Brainwashed: How Universities Indoctrinate America's Youth," "Porn Generation: How Social Liberalism Is Corrupting Our Future," and "Project President: Bad Hair and Botox on the Road to the White House." He has appeared on hundreds of television and radio shows around the nation, including "The O'Reilly Factor," "Fox and Friends," "In the Money," "DaySide with Linda Vester," "Scarborough Country," "The Dennis Miller Show," "Fox News Live," "Glenn Beck Show," "Your World with Neil Cavuto," "700 Club," "The Laura Ingraham Show," "The Michael Medved Show," "The G. Gordon Liddy Show," "The Rusty Humphries Show," "The Lars Larson Show," "The Larry Elder Show," The Hugh Hewitt Show," and "The Dennis Prager Show."

Facts & Furious
is also available as an e-book
for Kindle, Amazon Fire, iPad, Nook and
Android e-readers. Visit
creatorspublishing.com to learn more.

o o o

CREATORS PUBLISHING

We find compelling storytellers and
help them craft their narrative,
distributing their novels and collections
worldwide.

o o o

Made in the USA
Monee, IL
10 December 2024

72757185R00141